AF321684

State Composition and Collapse
of the Second Reich

State Composition and Collapse of the Second Reich

The Victory of the Bourgeois Citizen over the Soldier

Carl Schmitt

Edited and translated by Samuel Garrett Zeitlin

Foreword by Reinhard Mehring

polity

Originally published in German as *Staatsgefüge und Zusammenbruch des zweiten Reiches. Der Sieg des Bürgers über den Soldaten*. Copyright © 2011 Duncker & Humblot GmbH, Berlin. "Staatsgefüge und Zusammenbruch des zweiten Reiches" was first published in 1934 by the Hanseatischen Verlagsanstalt, Hamburg. "Die Logik der geistigen Unterwerfung" was first published in *Deutsches Volkstum*, 1 3. 1934, pp. 177–182.

This English translation © Polity Press, 2026

Polity Press
65 Bridge Street
Cambridge CB2 1UR, UK

Polity Press
111 River Street
Hoboken, NJ 07030, USA

ISBN-13: 978-1-5095-6624-2 hardback

A catalogue record for this book is available from the British Library.

Library of Congress Control Number: 2025941012

Typeset in 11 on 14 pt Adobe Caslon
by Cheshire Typesetting Ltd, Cuddington, Cheshire
Printed and bound in Great Britain by CPI Group (UK) Ltd, Croydon

The publisher has used its best endeavors to ensure that the URLs for external websites referred to in this book are correct and active at the time of going to press. However, the publisher has no responsibility for the websites and can make no guarantee that a site will remain live or that the content is or will remain appropriate.

Every effort has been made to trace all copyright holders, but if any have been overlooked the publisher will be pleased to include any necessary credits in any subsequent reprint or edition.

For further information on Polity, visit our website:
politybooks.com

Contents

Editor's Note and Acknowledgments

Writing in the *Historische Zeitschrift* in 2005, the German historian Dirk Blasius noted that "In the capacious Schmitt literature his treatise on the collapse of the Kaiserreich hardly receives any attention."[1] Several decades later, Blasius's judgment might be reiterated almost unaltered. Nonetheless, the present edition and translation have benefited substantially from Blasius's studies,[2] as well as the studies of Joshua Smeltzer, Lars Vinx, Günter Maschke, and Reinhard Mehring. It is thus fitting that this edition opens with a foreword by Professor Mehring.

This translation of Carl Schmitt's *State Composition and Collapse of the Second Reich* aims to produce as accurate a translation of Schmitt's German history within the limits of English readability, preserving Schmitt's paragraphing and sentence structure, the precision of Schmitt's political vocab-

[1] Dirk Blasius, "Carl Schmitt und der 'Heereskonflikt' des Dritten Reiches," *Historische Zeitschrift* 281 (2005), pp. 659–682, at p. 678: "In der umfangreichen Schmitt-Literatur findet seine Abhandlung über den Zusammenbruch des Kaiserreichs kaum Beachtung."

[2] Ibid. See also Dirk Blasius, *Carl Schmitt: Preußischer Staatsrat in Hitlers Reich* (Göttingen: Vandenhoeck & Ruprecht, 2001).

ulary, as well as the rhythm and tone of Schmitt's prose. The German term *Bürger*, present in Schmitt's subtitle and thematized throughout the book, does not distinguish between bourgeois and citizen, and for this reason *Bürger* is rendered throughout as "bourgeois citizen." A critic may argue that by "*Bürger*," Schmitt means "bourgeois" – which is not false. Yet, as Schmitt would go on to defend the Nuremberg Laws in 1935 (the year immediately after the publication of this book) and to persistently defend stripping Jews of their civic and citizenship rights in Germany (and in Nazi-occupied and allied lands), the concatenation of bourgeois and citizen within the term *Bürger* should not be effaced. Within Schmitt's political arguments from the 1930s, the soldier should triumph over the bourgeois, and a particular subset of those whom Schmitt inscribes as "bourgeois" are, from Schmitt's advocacy, to be stripped of citizenship and civic rights.[3]

The edition and translation was made on the basis of Günter Maschke's edition of Schmitt's German text (Berlin: Duncker & Humblot, 2011) checked against Schmitt's 1934 German original (Hamburg: Hanseatische Verlagsanstalt, 1934). Within the edition, Schmitt's own notes to the main text of *State Composition* and the Appendix are footnotes

---

[3] See Carl Schmitt, "Die Verfassung der Freiheit," *Deutsche Juristen-Zeitung* 40, no. 19 (1 October), Sp. 1133–1135, reprinted in Carl Schmitt, *Gesammelte Schriften 1933–1936* (Berlin: Duncker & Humblot, 2021), pp. 282–284. For Schmitt's defenses of the Vichy revocation of the Crémieux Decree in 1940, stripping Algerian Jews of their French citizenship, see Carl Schmitt, "The Forming of the French Spirit via the Legists," in Carl Schmitt, *The Tyranny of Values and Other Texts*, ed. Russell A. Berman and Samuel Garrett Zeitlin (Candor, NY: Telos Press, 2018), pp. 51–90.

to the main body of the text in Arabic numerals whilst the notes to the Foreword and the editorial notes are endnotes marked with Roman numerals.

For the chance to prepare this edition and translation for Polity, I am thankful to John Thompson and to Elise Heslinga and Evie Deavall, and to conversations with Susan Neiman.

Clara Maier and Martin Ruehl generously read the entire translation through and saved it from numerous errors. Those that remain are those of the translator.

At University College London, I am thankful for my colleagues in its storied department of History, Valentina Arena, Margot Finn, Alex Goodall, Angus Gowland, Fabian Krautwald, Patrick Lantschner, Sophie Page, Jason Peacey, Benedetta Rossi, John Sabapathy, Peter Schröder, Antonio Sennis, Julietta Steinhauer, Iain Stewart, and Florence Sutcliffe-Braithwaite. At the Institute for Historical Research, I am grateful for the chance to co-convene the "History of Political Ideas" seminar with Callum Barrell, Hannah Dawson, Andrew Fitzmaurice, Niall O'Flaherty, Angus Gowland, Dina Gusejnova, Humeira Iqtidar, Gareth Stedman Jones, Julia Nichols, Paul Sagar, Quentin Skinner, and Georgios Varouxakis.

Not least, I am thankful for the love of my family – to my sister, Ellie, my mother, Elizabeth, and my partner, Joanna.

The work of this translation is dedicated to Professors Valentina Arena, Angus Gowland, and Peter Schröder, with gratitude and intellectual esteem for their scholarship.

Samuel Garrett Zeitlin
University College London
London, 17 April 2025

"Spiritual Subjection"? On the "Tragic" Tone of Schmitt's Text

A Foreword to *State Composition and the Collapse of the Second Reich*

Reinhard Mehring

Schmitt's tight polemical text from early in the year 1934 is manifestly contemporary. Indeed, the questions concerning the relation between army and state, political constitution and military constitution, pose themselves anew after the "return of war" to Europe, in the Near East, and other regions of the world today, where the United States reorients itself toward a runoff with China and takes its distance from the "trans-Atlantic West." Everywhere in Europe, the European Union as well as NATO must newly adjust the mentality and constitution of state and society to military threats. Though it may sound odd, dissonant, crazy, or improbable, might a calculated National Socialist programmatic text by Carl Schmitt here be capable of stirring contemporary thought? Its critical questions concerning the "parliamentary army," "budgetary right," military service, and the constitutional weakening of political leadership and "unity" are, in any event, posed again today.

The brochure stands in a row of polemical and programmatic texts, which Schmitt published in swift succession after his decision for National Socialism: after the so-called Enabling Act (*Ermächtigungsgesetz*) of 24 March 1933, up until the summer of 1934 alongside a plethora of lectures, articles, and journal pieces.[i] If Schmitt was not only an opportunist and careerist, but rather a political author, constitutional theorist, and "thinker of order" who also disposed of fundamental answers and formational proposals, then this must show itself precisely in the programmatic brochures. As "crown jurist," Schmitt was already controversial in 1934: in April 1933, Schmitt, though not yet a member of the Nazi Party, was already participating as a legal-technical counselor in the formulation of the Reich Governors' Law (*Reichstatthaltergesetz*) for bringing the German states into line with Nazi policy, already lost in the course of the year 1933 as "state counsel" contact to Hermann Göring, and had to set himself more upon the *Reichsrechtsführer* Hans Frank, who did not belong among the first guard and the innermost circle with Hitler.

Schmitt's first programmatic text for the formation of the National Socialist *Führer*-state – *State, Movement, People* – remained extremely vague and recommended, according to the model of Göring's "state counsel," in terms of concrete constitutional politics little more than the erection of a "*Führer's* counsel" in parallel or as an alternative to the transmitted executive cabinet system; Hitler, however, persisted with the state and the Party. Up until the summer of 1934, Schmitt now wrote, from January 1934 onward, his brochures *On the Three Types of Juristic Thinking, State*

Composition and Collapse as well as *National Socialism and International Law*, which all grew out of lectures. Up until 30 June 1934 and the liquidation of the heads of the *Sturmabteilung* (SA), as well as one-time opponents of Hitler, with a portion of whom Schmitt was personally as well as politically connected; Schmitt then reacted with a ground-shaking alteration of perspective and of strategy, which he immediately signaled multivalently in a highly contested article, *Der Führer schützt das Recht* [*The Führer Protects the Law*]. Schmitt's hope for a constitutional capacity of National Socialism, and his exertions (in Schmitt's terminology) to elevate a state of exception into the normal condition of a strong "*Führer*-state," had failed. From then on, Schmitt saw himself again within the state of exception, viewing National Socialism as the Leviathan, and for further political-theological legitimation, grasped strengthened in the semantic arsenal of anti-Semitism and of apocalypticism.

State Composition and Collapse of the Second Reich is Schmitt's most thoroughgoing attempt to define the relation between state and movement of Hitler's "legal revolution." The text proceeds from a lecture on "Army Order and Complete Political Structure" ["Heerwesen und politische Gesamtstruktur"], which Schmitt held on 24 January in the aula of the Berlin University, repeated on 13 February at the urgent request of his fellow-traveler Carl Bilfinger[ii] in Halle, and which Schmitt promptly published in an abbreviated version under the title *The Logic of Spiritual Subjection* in the journal *Deutsches Volkstum*. Schmitt then rebuilt the text after the completion of *Three Types of Juristic Thinking* into the brochure. In his diary, Schmitt noted on 17 April, that, in the train en route "to Ernst Jünger and my godson" from Berlin to Goslar, he brought the manuscript "into order."[iii]

Since 1930, Schmitt was closely befriended with Ernst Jünger (1895–1998), a highly decorated war hero of the First World War, epitome of the idealized "Soldier." Jünger was an opponent of the Weimar Republic as well as of National Socialism. After a search raid on his house, Jünger withdrew from the firing line of Berlin to Goslar in December 1933. Despite the still-contrary assessment of National Socialism at the time, Jünger invited Schmitt[iv] to assume the godfathership of his second son Carl Alexander, whom Schmitt called a "new Earth soldier" in a congratulatory letter dated to 15 March 1934.[v] The *Hüter der Verfassung* [*Guardian of the Constitution*] had approvingly cited Jünger's "total mobilization"; *State Composition and Collapse* repeats this.[vi] In 1932, Jünger published his famous essay, *Der Arbeiter: Herrschaft und Gestalt* [*The Worker: Rule and Figure*],[vii] to which Schmitt responded with his discourse of the "Victory of the Bourgeois Citizen over the Soldier." *State Composition and Collapse* speaks without Jünger's stately confidence rather resignedly of an "opposition of human types": "*education and possession against blood and soil*," and of strife "concerning the figuration of the German himself."

The brochured series edited by Schmitt, *Der Deutsche Staat der Gegenwart* [*The Contemporary German State*], in which Schmitt's programmatic texts appear as volumes 1 and 6, Ernst Rudolf Huber published as volume 2, at that time the economic-legal sketch *Die Gestalt des deutschen Sozialismus* [*The Figuration of German Socialism*]. In a letter dated to 1 May 1934 addressed to Huber, Schmitt mentions a "difference of opinion concerning the concept of figure,"[viii] which refers to a "very deep philosophic question." By this, is perhaps meant the anthropological or characterological shaping force: whether military service or the industrial economy and factory shapes the "type" more. Schmitt does not assertively participate in the then-present controversies concerning philosophic anthropology, although he knew all the main participants – Max Scheler, Helmuth Plessner, Paul Ludwig Landsberg, Arnold Gehlen – closely; the *Concept of the Political* in particular approvingly referred to Plessner's text *Macht und menschliche Natur*. Fundamentally, however, Schmitt, like Jünger, shunned disciplinary controversies. Constitution in the absolute sense, it is said at the outset of *Constitutional Theory*, means "the concrete way of being given by itself with every existing political unity."[ix] It exists positively in the "self-assertion" of a political will, which, according to Schmitt's *Concept of the Political*, shows itself also and precisely in the military self-assertion and in "readiness for death and killing."[x] This will to political existence: distinction between friend and enemy, Schmitt finds missing in the German citizen, who, under the influence of "liberal thought," no longer desires to be a soldier, but rather descends into the "bourgeois" and consumer. The questions were already posed by Oswald Spengler at the outset of the Weimar Republic in his text *Preußentum und Sozialismus*.[xi] Behind this stands Nietzsche's question concerning the "Übermenschen" and the expressionistic search for the "new Menschen." From Spengler to Jünger the questions were posed against the "left" labor movement and Marxism. Hitler and National Socialism saw themselves in this line.

Schmitt's search for the constitution, type, and figure of a "strong" state is mostly discussed in scholarship from the vantage of the end and decline of the Weimar Republic and the role of the presidential system: often in the alternative Papen or Schleicher, although Schmitt sought proximity to both, while Brüning and the Catholic Center Party thoroughly ignored him. Here begin the riddles around the constitutional-political interpretation of Schmitt's polemical text from 1934: instead of the decline of the Weimar Republic, it considers the "collapse of the Second Reich" and thus makes Bismarck and the Kaiserreich co-responsible for the "collapse." Where, before the Leipzig State Court in the trial of *Preußen contra Reich* at the end of 1932, Schmitt had defended Papen's Reich executive action against the Social Democratic government of Prussia (the striking down of a situation of civil war via a Reich executive action Schmitt had already experienced in 1919), Schmitt now plays the "soldier state" and "Prussian honor" against the "dualistic" structure of the late Wilhelmine era, which, early in the year 1934, could be understood as opting for the Reichswehr against a "second revolution" (by the SA), but also as a warning about polycratic developments and about the failure of the "One Party State"[xii] in the construction of unity.

Is it really an historian who is writing here? Does Schmitt not rather argue for the present with an historical parallel? Does he thus warn in 1934 of a possible "collapse" of the "Third Reich"? In any event, the text is not tuned by "victory" but more by "spiritual subjection" and "collapse." Beyond the constitutional historical theses, fronts, and battles of 1934, the text in its pathos reads more like an historical drama or a tragedy of fate, for which, within Schmitt's canon, Grabbe, Hebbel, and Kleist may perhaps be named. One could read out of this a fascistic "aestheticization of politics,"[xiii] as Walter Benjamin diagnosed it almost simultaneously in the case of Italian futurism, whilst Schmitt, like other anti-bourgeois extremists of the interwar period, was more literarily shaped by German expressionism (Däubler).

Retrospectively, Schmitt swooned for the "tragic geniality of Hölderlin."[xiv]

With his *Concept of the Political*, Schmitt personalized and polemicized the political event. He speaks of "betrayal" and "spiritual subjection," "defensive" and "lost positions," of an "heroic path" and "decline."[xv] He declares the Minister of War to be a "tragic figure,"[xvi] and, indeed, even the Hitler-loyal Werner von Blomberg, Minister of War from 1933 to 1938, with whom Schmitt had spoken intensely "on the humanity of the soldier"[xvii] on 15 January 1934, was later dismissed under humiliating circumstances, to say nothing here of others like the Resistance of 20 July 1944. The "true causes of the catastrophe" Schmitt grounds in the "logic" of "spiritual subjection," which he fixes particularly "like the development of an illness" on "pathognomic moments" and "instances." The term of the "pathognomic moment" is, as a citation, placed in quotation marks without reference. What is meant is a set of symptoms without clear causes. Schmitt thus relativizes his pointed emphasis upon some decisions and withdraws them from intentional attribution and causal responsibility. Schmitt's interpretations of Bismarck's Indemnity Declaration have persistently irritated historians.[xviii] Schmitt, however, places it in a transpersonal "logic," treats the Indemnity Declaration more as a didactic example and symptom, and speaks of a "solely coherent line of development" and of a "law," which follows no natural causality, but rather an idealistic logic of "legal concepts": "first the inner political spiritual subordination of the Prussian soldier state under the legal concepts of the bourgeois civil rule-of-law and constitutional state; then the subjection under the spiritual war aim of the enemy . . .; and finally the open renunciation of the Prussian soldier state."[xix]

Schmitt's enemy in 1934 is not actually Versailles, Weimar, or Geneva, but rather "spiritual subjection" under a system of "liberal thought," as had already been criticized in the *Concept of the Political.*

Indeed, the brochure may be read as a *prise de parti* on behalf of the Reichswehr and as an appeal to the construction of political unity. After 30 June 1934, Schmitt also promptly justified the state murders as "rightful state necessity" of an "immediate justice,"[xx] which proclaimed legitimacy against legality. Yet the text also asks anew with tragically resigned tone and tenor about the politically existent "way of being" and the ruling "human type." After 1933, Ernst Jünger withdrew more into literature and in the following years wrote literarily significant works. Jünger's figurative vision of 1932 he poetized in a dystopian manner in an allegoric reckoning with National Socialism in 1938 with *On the Marble Cliffs.*[xxi] Schmitt replaced the alternative of "bourgeois citizen" and "soldier" later, with *Land and Sea*, via the distinction between a "maritime" and "terrestrial" political existence, and identified the "son of the earth" as the legitimate political actor finally in the "figure" of the "partisan," whom he positively elevated above the terroristic world-revolutionary.

At that time Schmitt glossed his personal copy of *State Composition and Collapse of the Second Reich*:[xxii] He expanded it with numerous references, pasted an early review from the *Berliner Tageblatt* of 7 June 1934 into his copy, but above all renamed the subtitle with light irony; the *Victory of the Bourgeois Citizen over the Soldier* now became *"The Victory of the Commodity [Ware] over the Weapon [Waffe] or: Bismarck's Legacy in the Reich Const[itution]!"* This refers to Max Weber's review[xxiii] of Erich Kaufmann's book on *Bismarck's Legacy in the Reich Constitution*. The wordplay of commodity [*Ware*] and weapon [*Waffe*] is provoked via the alliteration: perhaps Schmitt is not wholly serious that Bismarck is responsible for the turn of the bourgeois citizen to the world of consumption. Karl Marx, however, had already discovered or invented the peculiar logic of "Capital"; Schmitt now emphasizes a reification of political subjects. Some of his notes refer – next to other phases of work – to the year 1963, in which the *Theory of the Partisan* as well as the expanded last "edition" of *The Concept of the Political* appeared. In this year, Schmitt also glossed *State Composition and Collapse of the Second Reich* and thus linked or enmeshed the text, like a further "corollary," with his *Concept of the Political*. In the *Theory of the Partisan*, Schmitt significantly cites (without reference) a phrase of Hegel out of the *Phenomenology of Spirit*: "the weapons are the essence of the fighter himself."[xxiv] In Hegel, this allows itself to be marked as a "speculative proposition." Thus read, the new subtitle precisions and sharpens the discourse of the victory of the bourgeois citizen: when the consumption world of commodities steps into the place of weapons, there are no more soldiers.

In 1950 Schmitt published in the *Frankfurter Allgemeine Zeitung* a short article, *Der Mut des Geistes* [*The Courage of the Spirit*], which, parallel to recollections of Kleist's grave,[xxv] reads like a continuation of the tragedy of fate. Here, Schmitt links up with earlier observations out of *The Concept of the Political*: on "asceticism" as presupposition for the education of political elites.[xxvi] Now, however, he observes "possessive asceticism": immiseration and pauperization of the German bourgeois citizen via the World War as a "chance" for a new "hour of the phenomenology of spirit."[xxvii] In the Federal Republic, there has been renewed debate in recent years concerning "heroes"; Herfried Münkler[xxviii] intones that "posthistorical" industrial society is defenseless against the myths of martyrdom and the heroism of Islamic fundamentalism and terrorism. Beyond the constitutional questions, Schmitt's text is also such a critical analysis of mentalities; it asks not only about "state composition" and the "constituent power" (Huber)[xxix] of the military constitution, but also concerning the political will to the constitutional decision concerning "ways of being" and forms of life. In a strong reading, one could mark this, with Aristotle, as a basic question of political philosophy.

State Composition and Collapse of the Second Reich

The Victory of the Bourgeois Citizen over the Soldier

CONTENTS

I. PRUSSIAN SOLDIER STATE AND BOURGEOIS CIVIL CONSTITUTIONALISM

For Prussia, the leading German state, the bourgeois-liberal development of the nineteenth century signified a time of constant open or concealed conflicts between government and parliament. In typical fashion, the conflicts touched upon the *army* and the *state budget*. Government and parliament, state and society, army and economy, soldier and bourgeois citizen stood in the complete composition of "constitutional" Prussia in an opposition, which, after the founding of the *Reich* transferred itself to the German *Reich* and had to cleft it, politically and spiritually, into two parts. Out of the inner cleft of its state organization, out of the inconspicuous, but inexorable, logic of state-constructive consequentiality, dangers arose to the Prussian state and therewith to the German *Reich*, the consciousness of which declined, first, in the ecstasy of economic prosperity, and, then, in the frantic hope of its restoration.

The state- and constitutional thought of the nineteenth century endures into the present. The after-effects of an almost century-long cleft are very strong and enduring, with the hardly vanquishable power of spiritual-intellectual "residues." Decisive concepts, like constitution, freedom and equality, rule-of-law state and statute, rule with particular ideal notions both the image of history as well as the state- and constitutional thought of the whole last century. They have created in this enduring conflict between soldier and citizen numerous fixed, graspable concepts and formulae and constructed the confrontation between army and constitution, state and society, politics and economics as an enduring state of affairs. They have, in particular, hindered the ordering of the German worker into the Second *Reich* founded by Bismarck. Only since the victory of the National Socialist movement is there the possibility of overcoming the constitutional concepts of bourgeois social thought via another complete state structure, the triadic unity of state, movement, people, and of hindering the – immediately wholly self-evident – restoration of the state system which *Adolf Hitler*[i] in his parliamentary speech on 30 January 1934 labeled as [a] "bourgeois-legitimist compromise."

The German people has soldierly qualities like few other peoples. In the soldier state Prussia the German people created a political figuration[ii] of this essential type [*Wesensart*] and thereby made possible the continuance of the German people as a political unity. First in the Prussian kingship, then in the Prussian General Staff, the Prussian soldier state found the form and leadership [*Führung*], which were measured to its concrete type [*Art*] of political existence. But from the beginning this soldier state stood in danger either of falling into a spiritual stricture and mere defensive, or, however, of succumbing to a foreign spirit. Already under Frederick the Great the deepest thinker of the Prussian East, *Johann Georg Hamann*, appealed in a touching and gripping way from the "Philosopher of Sanssouci" to the "King of Prussia."[iii,1] Throughout the whole nineteenth century, however, a soldierly people and a soldier state stood internally helpless against the claims to political power of a wholly self-evident *bourgeois-liberal* constitutional and rule-

---

[1] In his writing (composed in the French language) to the General Administration of the Tolls of 18 August 1776 (in Gildemeister's edition of Hamann's *Leben und Schriften*, Bd. II., p. 202).

of-law state. What the Freiherr vom Stein had written to the Crown Prince Friedrich Wilhelm can – detached from the situation of the year 1822 – almost hold as a leading proposition of the complete development up until 1933: "Finally the military and the bourgeois civic institutions stand in contradiction with one another. These paralyze the common spirit, those presuppose it."[2]

The Prussian General Staff, in its two-hundred-year history, endured victories and defeats. It did not decline into that lowly ecstasy, to which after the victorious wars of 1866 and 1870, in an age of apparently boundless booming economic upswing, whole orders and generations of the German people succumbed. It was able to accommodate itself to the monstrous dimensions of a modern World War, even showed itself to be up to them and brought forth a field commander of the world-historical grandeur of *Ludendorff*. But the misrelation and the inner, spritual cleft between state-leading and war-leading, the fruitful dualism of the inner-state composition of Prussia and therewith also of the *Reich*, were finally still stronger than everything, which the soldierly force of the German army and the wonder-worthy grandeur of its military leadership could bring to fulfillment in four years of war. It is high time to recognize this clearly. A still thoroughgoingly dominant national-liberal image of history and a state doctrine bound up with it and born out of the same spirit have hindered us till now from delving down into the deepest and most authentic causes of the collapse of 1918. Yet we must not cease to ask after the true causes of the calamity, so that the path remains free and the right goal

---

[2] *Bemerkungen über die allgemeinen Grundsätze des Planes zu einer provin-zial-ständischen Verfassung*, Kappenberg, am 5. November 1822.

remains recognizable. I shall attempt to fulfill this duty with help of the insights and results of my academic discipline, not in order to throw up new questions of guilt and to name new guilty culprits, but rather in order to uncover the veils of a liberal state law doctrine which has been dominant for two generations, to see aright the state composition of the Second *Reich* in its real constitution, and thereby to raise to the consciousness of contemporary Germany both the dangerous ripping asunder of army and constitution, state and society, as well as also the fatal antagonism between stately-military and civil-societal bourgeois leadership.

1.

The conflict between waging war[iv] [*Kriegführung*] and politics, which caused Germany's collapse, attains its authentic depth via a complete state structure clefted in itself, which stems wholly from the liberal nineteenth century. The liberal movement of the year 1848 compelled the Prussian state to accept a "constitution" and expose itself to the danger of losing its very essence, in that its government would become parliamentary and its army a parliamentary army. Despite all reservations and distinctions, despite the so-to-speak official distinction between constitutional and parliamentary government, this was the logical final consequence of that which one understood at the time under a "constitution." A "constitutional" government was ultimately only a parliamentary government. Thus in 1848 it was first understood,[3]

---

[3] Compare Fritz Hartung, *Verantwortliche Regierung, Kabinette und Nebenregierungen im konstitutionellen Preußen 1848–1918, Forschungen zur brandenburgischen und preußischen Geschichte*, XLIV, Heft 1, p. 2 f.

before one clasped the juristic straw husk of that distinction between "parliamentary" and "constitutional"; thus it became apparent in the still unresolved constitutional conflict, which entered immediately, as soon as the Prussian solider state reflected upon itself and upon its army.

The Prussian constitutional conflict from 1862 to 1866 let the irresolvable problem of a compromise between the German soldier state and the bourgeois civil constitutional state to emerge unveiled for a brief time. For our contemporary constitutional legal and state constructive consciousness this conflict tends ever more toward a boiling point of an inner state problematic, to a process, which, like the "pathognomic moment" in the development of an illness, suddenly allows in a moment the otherwise concealed true condition to be recognized. It is the central event of internal German history of the last century.[4] It displayed, in place of the veiling, untrue exaggeration of the distinction between constitutional and parliamentary government, the essential opposition between soldier and liberal bourgeois citizen. In some form, it periodically repeated itself with every later military bill, with every great political turn and with symptomatic particularities, as in the Saverne affair 1913.[v] Finally it also essentially defined the Weimar constitution, which in wide measure is nothing other than the delayed answer to the inner political question of this great conflict.

The constitutional conflict of 1862–1866 was a military conflict and a budget conflict simultaneously. The conflict related to the army organization and its financing, and thereby

---

[4] From Paul *Ritterbusch* a representation of the central constitutional historical and state theoretical significance of the Prussian constitutional conflict is to be expected.

the conflict gripped the two essential competencies of every, and in particular, of the Prussian, state: army and finance, war and economy. It only seemingly ended with a compromise. The kingly government put through the army reform against the will of the Prussian *Landtag* and won two wars, yet after the victories it sought retroactive recognition, approval and release, "*indemnity*" from the parliament and received it. The decisive passage of the speech, with which the King opened the Prussian *Landtag* on 5 August 1866, reads thus:

> "The state expenditures, which have been made in this time, lack the legal basis, which the state budget receives, *as I repeatedly recognize*, only via Article 99 of the constitutional instrument annually between my government and both houses of the *Landtag* by agreed upon statute. The administration of the previous year without this foundation sprang from a *situation of necessity*, which made it wholly impossible for the government to act otherwise, but now shall not persist further."

Here it is not a matter of how the leading men, be it the King, Bismarck or another, grounded and justified this step in its particulars to themselves, whether the request for indemnity was a "confession of injustice committed," a "*pater peccavi*"[vi] or not, whether it was only a "formal discharge" without "worse consequences" or ought to have been something else.[5] The dominant, one may say "official"

---

[5] On this the 21st chapter of Bismarck's *Gedanken und Erinnerungen* and in particular the article in the *Hamburger Nachrichten* from 21 June 1891 (Hermann Hofmann, *Fürst Bismarck 1890–1898*, Bd. 1, Stuttgart 1913, p. 370), which in any event stems from a time in which Bismarck placed particular value on not being held to be an opponent of the parliament. On Bismarck's motives compare below p. 26.

constitutional legal doctrine gave the answer that there was a *gap in the constitution.*[vii] *"Here, state law ceases."*[viii],[6] Therewith it was recognized that the state still didn't really have a constitution. As the essential question was not encompassed by the constitution, and the gap set in precisely in the decisive case, whose answering for both partners of the constitutional agreement had to be the actual content of the constitution. Nobody was conscious of the abysmal double meaning of the proposition "Here, state law ceases." The constitutional conflict ended without decision. Each could hold itself as the internal political victor and could proceed for further confrontation on the basis that it defended and enacted its good right. The conflict was not ended, not even by an authentic material compromise; it was only with the help of a wholly extraordinary external political success in an extraordinary situation, in the mood after a victorious war, concealed and surmounted, i.e. to a later and another time delayed. Every subsequent army bill showed that the decisive question, touching on army and budget, was still open. The "constitution" of Prussia and of the Second *Reich*, like the whole so-called "constitutionalism," thus gave in the decisive point no solution at all, above all no authentic compromise solution in the matter. For the soldier state Prussia, it was a deceptive win to be a "constitutional state" and to have placed the principle of its political existence in question for the pottage of lentils[ix] of a foreign legality.[x]

[6] G. *Anschütz* in the text book of state law by Meyer-Anschütz, seventh edition, 1919, p. 906. That the gap theory uncloaked the true constitutional situation and that the gap was fundamental, shows itself also in the attempt of Freiherr *Marschall* von *Bieberstein* to place the lack of countersignature by orders of the highest warlord in parallel with the lack of budgetary approval: in *Verantwortlichkeit und Gegenzeichnung bei Anordnungen des Obersten Kriegsherrn* (Berlin, 1911), p. 431.

The Prussian constitution of 1850 attempted to bind a military and civil service state together with a bourgeois civil constitutional state. It was not agreed upon by the internal political partners, but rather one-sidedly authorized by the King, but it could be conceived as a compromise to the extent that the one part, the King, had yielded. It was, at least, an apparent compromise. The constitutions of the North German Confederation of 1867 and of the German *Reich* of 1871 were already "agreed upon" with the parliament. As partners of the apparent compromise the Prussian military monarchy and the liberal bourgeois movement clearly stood against one another. Upon this was grounded the dualistic structure of the thus emergent state composite. The army remained the core of the Prussian state; it was not only, as oft was said, a "state within the state"; it was *the* state within the state. But with regard to it liberal-bourgeois state law ceased. The civil service, which after 1807 still had fulfilled the task of a leading and state-bearing class, was "objectified" and "neutralized"; according to the basic principle of the "lawfulness of the executive" it was subjected to the "statute," i.e. subjected to a political will only arising under the collaboration of an agreement of the popular representative. It remained in its disposition loyal to the King, but only within the frame of the legality of a rule-of-law and constitutional state, in which the *lex* and not the *rex*, a norm and not a *Führer* gave the measure. It lost the political nerve and therewith also the capacity of being the state-bearing class of the political unity of the German people.[7] As a consequence

---

[7] Otto *Hintze* wrote in the year 1901 (*Acta Borussica*, Die Behördenorganisation und die allgemeine Staatsverwaltung Preußens im 18. Jahrhundert, Bd. VI, p. 554): "The bureaucracy of 1740 was an

of the securities of the rule-of-law state in addition to its ancillary position as well as its legal proprietary claims, in the course of the nineteenth century in the battle of the liberal bourgeoisie against the Prussian soldier state the civil service attained a type of intermediate position.[8] Between the civil service and the monarch stood the statute and a norming document, the constitution. Not to the King, but rather to a system of norms, was the civil servant sworn by oath (compare Article 108 of the Prussian constitution of 1850), whilst the soldier carried out his oath of allegiance to his King. In the confrontation between the Prussian soldier state and bourgeois civil society, the "liberal privy council [*Geheimrat*]," according to its education and its objective situation, was in no way the spiritual ally of the soldier state.

---

ecclesia militans, was a reform party in the state itself, which with the ideas of the Enlightenment and of equality before the law, with the new cameralistic education fought a rotten society and its egoistic views. The contemporary bureaucracy is no longer an *ecclesia militans*; it has long since conquered, it no longer wishes to fight; it has comfortably established itself and occupies itself with the conservative task of defending its old inherited possessive order against uncomfortable innovations; but as an order . . . as closed body it no longer stands so distant from the peak of the times and its education, as the bureaucracy did in the past."

[8] The early liberal "peculiar proximity of the battle against the bureaucracy and battle for the securing of its legal position" is treated by Th. Wilhelm, *Die Idee des Berufsbeamtentums* (Tübingen, 1933), p. 11f.: "Via the constitutional securing of the legal position of the civil service, the civil service itself is turned from being a tool of the monarch and made into a stricture upon the government. From there it is only a short step to fully turning the skewer around and making the weapon of the government against the 'people' into a weapon 'of the people' against the government inimical to the people."

If one holds before one's eyes the authentic state reality, namely the soldierly character of the Prussian monarchy, then the internally essentially foreign aspect of this combination of state and bourgeois civil society, this whole "bourgeois-legitimist compromise" becomes visible. The southern German states were not in the same measure as Prussia the bearers of a particular historical mission, grounded in the soldierly character of the state. They could regard the compromise as a dangerless resort. Their monarchs could be good bourgeois civil kings as long as they did not for their individual persons, like the noble King Ludwig II of Bavaria, go to the ground on the existential contradictions of a bourgeois-legitimist princely existence. In Prussia, however, the so-called "constitutional" system was only a veil over the abyss, which separates forever a Prussian soldier state from a liberal bourgeois civil state. The dualism of soldier and citizen was here not somehow a case of the peaceful division of functions and competences, no dividing "equalization," no *juste milieu*, no somehow "balancing equipoise" of prince and people, government and parliament. The opposition was also deeper than that between a general state bourgeois citizen and of a special service and power relation of the kind of the civil service. It is indicative in the highest degree for the bourgeois civil doctrine of state law of the Second *Reich*, that it sought to interpret the "peculiar relations between the soldier and the state" as a mere modification of the civil service relationship, as a "power relation" not essentially different from that one, "only that the duty of military obedience has a greater scope and is secured via stricter punishments from violation." This "*Laband's* sharp eye recognized immediately".[9] In this

---

[9] Compare Freiherr *Marschall* von *Bieberstein, op. cit.*, p. 359.

way, the public legal theory contributed to transforming the soldier into a civil servant, to take from him his essential type of being and thereby to imbricate him within the legal system of the bourgeois civil constitutional state. But neither the mediating position of the civil service secured by the rule-of-law state, nor partisan intermediate constructs like National Liberals or Free Conservatives were able to surmount the opposition. Indeed, soldier and liberal bourgeois citizen, Prussian army and bourgeois civil society, are oppositions simultaneously of world-view, of spiritual and moral education, of legal thought and above all also of the fundamental points of departure for the state structure and organization.

A *Führer-state* [*Führerstaat*] built by German soldiers can conclude no authentic compromise with a *rule-of-law state* [*Rechtsstaat*] built by the liberal bourgeois citizenry. Since 1848 it has no longer been a matter of the old opposition between line and land army, also not concerning the alteration between a conservative and a liberal government and the differences of a "regime," but a matter of the infinitely deeper antagonism between essentially different human types. It was a matter of the figure of the German himself, down into his physical peculiarities. A constitutional "compromise" organized and stabilized the inner cleft between a doubly contradictory army and state constitution: by force of the right to vote the Prussian voted for his "popular representative" as "bourgeois citizen" according to liberal and ultimately according to liberal democratic precepts; by force of the general military duty he was a soldier and totally immersed by the Prussian people's army in the decisive years of his life and in the decisive times of his being. The compound term "state citizen" ["*Staatsbürger*"] (a compromise variant of the term "world citizen" ["*Weltbürger*"]) veils the problem like other word-couplings typical for the national-liberal cleft, e.g. "federal state" ["*Bundesstaat*"] or "rule-of-law state" ["*Rechtsstaat*"]. When King Wilhelm I, with the entire security of his Prussian state sense, fought for the three-year military service period, and passed it down to his successors as an holy testament, he thus recognized the significance of precisely this third year of military service, as well as the state principle at its foundation, for which he fought: only in the third year of military service did the total immersion via the soldier state enter in, the internal transformation into the Prussian soldier, who distinguished himself from a militarily instructed bourgeois citizen.

Behind the dualism between Prussian soldier state and the bourgeois civil constitutional state there thus stood something Other and Deeper[xi] than the general internal political battle concerning the "government." This dualism rooted itself in the insurmountable *opposition between mutually contradictory, total claims to leadership, education and training.* Via the development toward liberal state citizens was the *opposition of human types*, the opposition of *education and possession against blood and soil* became visible. The advancing German *worker* sharpened the problematic. Although the worker possessed all the characteristics of the German, he placed himself under foreign leadership. The worker thereby became the tool of the actual usufructuaries of liberal constitutionalism, namely of Catholic Center and international Marxist politics, in their battle against Bismarck's Prusso-German *Reich*.

2.

The Prussian soldier state defended itself courageously.[xii] It was able to achieve the enactment of making the oath of allegiance to the lord of the land rather than to the constitution, and thereby to allow the army to manifest itself as the followership of a *Führer*. It was further able to make the military supreme command [*Kommandogewalt*] free from the constitutional requirement of ministerial countersignature. Thereby the army was taken out of the domain of the bourgeois civil constitutional system and as a kingly or kaiserly army it was defended from becoming a parliamentary army. Also in the strife over the scope of the supreme command [*Kommandogewalt*], in particular over the requirement of ministerial countersignature for the naming and dismissal of officers and over military justice, Prussia upheld its standpoint well. The army was thus withdrawn from the political consequences of the liberal constitutional state.

The doctrine of state law came to terms with the fact that orders of the supreme commander[xiii] were not countersigned by the "responsible" Minister of War. One had different constructions for the justification of Prussian practice: customary law, nature of the matter and particularly, after *Hecker's* article in Stengel's *Dictionary* of 1890,[xiv] the distinction between governmental power [*Regierungsgewalt*] and supreme command [*Kommandogewalt*]. It is in any case of the greatest symptomatic significance that the only thoroughgoing monographic treatment of the question in state law, the treatise, which was very successful in the doctrine of state law, appearing in the year 1911 by Freiherr *Marschall* von *Bieberstein*, with the whole high-handedness of strictly "juristic" – that was, for it, self-evidently bourgeois civil constitutional state – thought, took up the proof that the constitution made *all* orders of the supreme commander duty-bound for a countersignature and that all orders that were not countersigned were accordingly unconstitutional and errant. Only because the soldier possessed a restricted right of review and on account of the peculiarity of military obedience, on account of the "absolute service power" of the supreme commander, should these errant acts nonetheless be binding and must compulsorily be followed; admittedly only by soldiers, not by military civil servants and other persons not bound to military obedience. This book is for the intellectual situation of both the Prussian soldier state as well as the doctrine of state law of the German pre-War period acutely indicative. Its result runs (p. 435):

> "A juristic justification of such (not countersigned) orders with regard to the constitutional command set against them is renounced from the very beginning – as our science is not there to transmit the desired legal legitimation to political pos-tulates, but rather, on the contrary, to direct such postulates toward their legal restrictions, wherein our science strives only to grasp and to explain juristically the existing condition of law with its means and forms. The legal explanation of the factually present efficacy of these errant and yet not negligible acts out of a restriction of the right of review based upon the increased subjection of certain organs has then led wholly of itself simultaneously to the *bounding* of this efficacy and indeed to the fixing of a personal domain of effect."

"Legally" and "juristically" the whole Prussian practice, with all naming of officers and military tribunal orders by the Kaiser, was thus unconstitutional and errant; but because the right of review of the soldier with regard to illegal orders is restricted, the German soldier had nonetheless to obey! I hold that a state based upon its army, in which such a type of jurisprudence is held to be "unpolitical," is hollowed out and ordained to decline.

But not only the liberal science of state and constitutional law, the whole intellectual development pressed the Prussian soldier state into a difficult defensive. Liberal democracy pushed forth in the nineteenth century outside of Germany, in Europe and in the whole world, as well as within Germany with destined irresistibility. Many observers already expected in the first half of the century that it would rupture this dam. Under such aspects, the Prussian soldier state appeared only as an already overflooded island, whose fate was sealed. Liberalism and democracy felt themselves sure of the future upon the side of progress, of freedom, of development, of the coming things, and the Marxist social democracy thronged after in the self-same direction along the like thought-paths. In the historical image of the liberal century the development line of humanity took its course from the militaristic to the industrial type, from war to peace, from politics to the economy, from institutional establishment to comradery, from absolutism to democracy. Not only for the Church Father of this liberal metaphysic, *H. Spencer*, was precisely Prussia – next to Dahomey, the Incan Empire, Russia and similar mythic images of terror – a militaristic state of violence. As the exact intellectual historical parallel to the Weimar constitution and as the foundation of its world-view, this myth of Prussian militarism and its counter-image, of Anglo-Saxon peaceful commercialism, were openly proclaimed "scientifically" even in Germany in the year 1919 (in *Joseph Schumpeter's* "Sociology of Imperialisms"). This lay in the consequential logic of liberal-bourgeois thought. Not even a well-intentioned "monarchist" reservation of a patriotic national liberal could restrain the course of this logic. Intellectually, or rather – to use the word adequate to it – ideologically, the liberal movement, despite the misadventure of its revolution of 1848 and despite its own reservations, grasped with the greatest self-evidence, even in Germany, all the domains of public life. The example of the southern German states, in which constitutionalism appeared to be paradigmatically successful and even the supreme command [*Kommandogewalt*] was subjected to countersignature in its full ambit according to the liberal-constitutional demand, could serve as a particularly striking argument. Even during the World War, the representatives of the later Weimar Coalition drove home the validity of the claim that the Bavarian, Württemberg, and Saxon officers named under countersignature of the minister were just as courageous and loyal soldiers as the Prussian officers.

In such a situation the liberal argumentation had the great political preponderance, which the possession of a politically contested concept creates. *Constitutional state* [*Verfassungsstaat*] and *rule-of-law state* [*Rechtsstaat*] were their monopoly. They created their own concepts of law and constitution, and everything, which they did and demanded, thus appeared as a battle, not somehow for a liberal law and a liberal constitution, for a liberal rule-of-law state and liberal freedom and equality, but rather for *the* constitution and *the* rule-of-law state, for freedom and equality simply. Unforeseen everywhere, even in the presentations of the Prussian government, the word "constitution" was attributed a liberal rule-of-law state sense. When the supreme command in Prussia was excepted from ministerial countersignature and was thereby exempted from the liberal part of the state constitution, this had to manifest itself for that which Prussia held to be its true constitution, for the modes of thought and speech of the bourgeois civil constitutional state as a condition not at all encompassed by the constitution, as a constitutionless, anarchic, impossible condition. During the consultation about the Reich's Military Statute, 1874, the National Liberal *Führer* von Bennigsen: "The war constitution, the institution of the army build such an essential component part of the constitution of a people, of a state, they build up to so high a measure the skeleton of the constitution of every state, that, if it is not possible, ... to harmonize the army constitution and the military constitution into the constitutional constitution –, the constitution in such a land has still not yet become a true reality at all." The forceful and powerful Prussian soldier state lacked the intellectual power over the legal concepts of its age and over the newly constructed legal notions of the nineteenth century. *Roon* wrote in 1865: "Our opponents are unhindered in taking the initiative ... Yet the advantages of the initiative are in the battle of the spirits as in the battle of weapons equally decisive."[10] The well-known antitheses of law against power, rule-of-law state [*Rechtsstaat*] against power-state [*Machtstaat*], constitution against arbitrariness worked of themselves *against* the Prussian soldier state. Also the antitheses of spirit against power, education against the lack thereof, worked for the liberal, bourgeois civil society and against the Prussian state. The propagandistic

---

[10] Letter to Perthes of 3 June 1865, *Denkwürdigkeiten* (5. Aufl., Berlin 1905), vol. 2, p. 345; the expressions of von Bennigsen in the stenographic Reichstag's reports [*Stenogr. Reichstagsberichten*] 1874, Bd. 2, p. 41.

juxtaposition of the peace-loving, possessing and educated bourgeois citizen against power-hungry, uneducated and unintellectual Prussian militarism is only the coarsest but also the most consequential case of the application of this general dualism. The whole liberal litany of rule-of-law state against police state, popular state against authoritarian state, comradery against establishment, constitution against dictatorship, intellect and education against militarism enacted itself in its way of speaking and thinking in the most diverse levels of intellectual and societal life. It also penetrated into the juristic education of the civil servants and dominated the intellectual atmosphere. The complaint against the jurists of Germany, to which even Rudolf Gneist (*Der Rechtsstaat*, p. 149) saw himself occasioned, holds not only for the time of the early liberalism up to 1848, the "constitutional" mode of thought endures much more into the present and documents itself in numerous decisions of the courts, in particular of the State Court for the German *Reich* as well. Gneist speaks of the "ripping propaganda" of constitutional ideas and says: "In this circle of ideas the jurists of Germany also took their part, not so much with the particular knowledge of their profession, as with the *general education and with the societal notions*, which they had in common with the educated classes of the German people. The peculiar conglomeration of our private and criminal law and the narrow interest, which the vanished *Reich* state law offered to legal studies, habituated our jurists to a constant division between 'theory and practice'. The whole state law was reckoned by the judge and attorney to 'theory', i.e. it fell prey to the most free-floating individual notion, in which the *Prussian jurist as well* (unencumbered with his Part II of the General Land Law) *vied with the state-philosophy of the educated classes*. The doctrines of French constitutionalism now found upon all sides a ready soil and now appeared in the philosophic garment so appealing to us as a 'General State Law' [*,allgemeines Staatsrecht*']. This it was which one so gladly heard in the Universities."

An Eduard Lasker thus stood leading [*führend*] upon the side of spirit, law and education against men like Bismarck, Moltke and Roon, who consequently stood upon the side of the uneducated. This type, not the great German men, would define the "constitution" of the German *Reich*! What bewilderment! The removal of the supreme command [*Kommandogewalt*] out of the liberal constitutional system, i.e. the salvation of German soldiery from the claims to leadership of such a type [*Art*] of "education," appeared to all these bourgeois citizens as an ungraspable abnormity, as incomprehensible hardheadedness of an evil militarism, which was posited as an enemy of freedom, as the last bulwark of a reaction inimical to spirit, education and progress. In his famed letter to Herr von Vincke of 2 January 1863,[11] King Wilhelm I, to whom this whole conceptual play ripping apart state and law and state and constitution was ungraspable, asked with the indignation of a legally thinking man: "Where does it state in the Constitution that only the government ought to make concessions and the legislative deputies never???" The answer to this question, which the King supplied with three question marks, lay in the fact that the constitutional concept of the nineteenth century was precisely the liberal constitutional concept of the bourgeois civil "popular representative," and this had the "spirit of the time" upon its side. To it the kingly government gave over the intellectual battlefield via its request for indemnity.

---

[11] Printed in Bismarck's *Gedanken und Erinnerungen*, [I] 14th chapter.

In a state with such a concept of constitution, the soldierly part of the state stood upon a lost position. The constitution itself, the basic law, the basic agreement, the fundamental "compromise," was concluded exclusively at the cost of the soldier state. In the German nineteenth century, in material fact, "constitution" meant essentially not somehow only a restriction of kingly power competencies, but rather above all a negation of the bases and consequences of the Prussian soldier state. This was the inner basic law, according to which monarchic constitutionalism emerged in Prussia and under which it had to further develop itself with inevitable logic. A state- or constitutional court, before the victory of 1866, would have sided in law with these liberals and hindered Bismarck's *Reich*. The originary compromise, which such a constitution represented, had to sustain itself with ever further compromises of the same structure, with ever further diminutions of the soldier state. Every statute, every annual budget, every army bill, every agreement between the government and parliament on the strength of the military presence in peacetime and similar occasions, confirmed and expanded the power of the popular representative over the constitution and transmitted to it, even when it yielded and accommodated the government, new arguments and new legal titles. Every concession, within the logic of such a constitutional situation, to the military demands of the government endangered the parties that were willing to make them, and made them defenseless against the cheap trumps of the "Left" parties, who had the logic of the bourgeois constitutional state upon their side. The law of development to which the Prussian soldier state had entered into, when it entered into this type of "constitution," could only work itself out *against* the Prussian soldier state. Tremendous military and foreign policy successes altered nothing in this, and could only effect a deferral, a delay. Victorious wars, the likes of which world-history seldom knows, political successes of the most astounding type only helped this Prussian soldier state needily to assert its existence, to conceal the conflict, to achieve the exemption of the supreme command and a veiling of the open conflict. On this, the external luster of this time should not deceive. A parliament, which had done everything in order to make the victory impossible, against whose loud cry and open contradiction the army organization operated successfully and the victory was achieved, was beseeched by the victor for indemnity and sanctioned the victorious war.

King Wilhelm the First recognized the decisive point of the fraught situation of the Prussian state, the military supreme command [*Kommandogewalt*], and upheld it with heroic fixity. The more that both the particularities and backgrounds of the history of the battle between the Prussian soldier state and the liberal movement become known to us, the more the figure of this King grows into a world-historical grandeur. His superiority was noiseless. It was not the superiority of an ingenious individual, but rather the superiority of a man integrated into the super-individual historical context, who holds fast to a line, which was only recognizable to him by force of his self-evident unity with the Prussian state. In a century which was filled with the noise of liberal constitutional legal discussions, he heard only the voice of the duty to the state, and, namely to the Prussian soldier state. Only thereby did he find the force to retain the great and ingenious men, who brought the work to fulfillment: Bismarck, Moltke and Roon. But even the King pressed for beseeching the parliament for "indemnity" after the victorious war. This was precisely "constitutional correctness."

3.

Bismarck himself thoroughly laid out the grounds which moved him to seek after "Indemnity" in the 21st chapter of his *Gedanken und Erinnerungen*.[xv] For him it was a matter of winning over the liberal opposition of the Prussian Landtag, of taking away an effective weapon from the numerous "unsatisfied persons" in old Prussia, in the newly acquired provinces and in the rest of Germany and of keeping in hand "the leadership upon liberal and national territory." No one will deny that this was a convincing ground. It would be foolhardy to retrospectively come to rights with Bismarck or even somehow to give right to the conservative reaction of this time. Nonetheless it is necessary to look the experiences in the eye, which in the course of the further development also yielded for Bismarck himself that an internal political decision was lacking.

Precisely this passage in Bismarck's *Gedanken und Erinnerungen* is full of restrictions and reservations. Bismarck says of the Prussian constitution: "It's possible to govern with it." But he says this expressly *after* the victorious war and immediately adds: "*Before* the war I would not have spoken of indemnity, now after the war the King was in the situation to grant it magnanimously." For him it is thus remarkably the King, who grants the indemnity. Therein is shown that each of the inner political opponents could believe themselves not only to be in the right, but also still able to grant something to the other: the King "grants" the request for indemnity, and the Landtag "grants" the indemnity. In the immediate additive to this sentence Bismarck then seeks simultaneously to render the whole occasion harmless and to frame it as a mere strife about words, about linguistic and juristic matters lacking an object. He speaks of a "linguistic and legal error," intones that it was now a matter of "building a golden bridge, whether politically or linguistically" to the inner political opponents to the extent that they were national and not only liberal and then concludes his remarks with a Latin citation that goes in the same direction and diminishes the whole problem of indemnity into a strife about words: *In verbis simus faciles.*[xvi]

Bismarck internally never fell into the mode of thought of the liberal rule-of-law and constitutional state. In any event, only later did he clearly recognize the authentic sense and the political dangers of the ideology and of the term "rule-of-law state," in the experiences of the battle with the Center Party and Social Democracy. Now, namely, it emerges that a battle over words and concepts, according to the changing political situation, can become a consequential political occasion out of a mere "linguistic and legal" one. In a text addressed to Goßler of 25 November 1881 *Bismarck* says: "I admittedly share the concern that we thereby (namely via an expansion of the full powers of the government) thereby *will fall into lively battle with the artificial expression invented by Robert von Mohl of the 'rule-of-law state',* of which there is still no definition satisfactory to a political head and no translation into any other language."[12] Yet in the year 1866 he felt

---

[12] For the reference to this thoroughgoingly important *prise de position* by Bismarck to the term and concept of the rule-of-law state [*Rechtsstaat*] I thank my esteemed colleague Professor Johannes *Heckel*, who discovered and published it in his treatise "Die Beilegung des Kulturkampfes in Preußen" ["The Settlement of the Culture War in Prussia"] (*Zeitschrift der Savigny-Stiftung für Rechtsgeschichte, Kanonistische Abteilung* XIX, 1930, p. 268ff.). In order to understand the sense of the battle concerning a term like "*Rechtsstaat*" or "*Verfassungsstaat*"

himself to be too much the victor to already place the possibility of a political danger of such terms into the reckoning. At that time he wished and was able "to throw into the pan" the request for indemnity, similar to the introduction of the general right to vote. Thereby he incidentally recognized the whole process thoroughly as what it really was, namely as a "delaying of the inner questions." Expressly he presupposes that one must first clarify the foreign policy situation and make oneself independent of foreign countries, because only then "in our own inner development could we move freely, where we can then institute ourselves as liberally or as reactionarily, as seems just and purposive." The further course of the inner political development has shown that the logic of liberal constitutionalism redounded to the benefit of the powers of a pluralistic party state, in particular to the political Catholicism of the Center and to Social Democracy. In the year 1866 and in the constitution of 1871 one had first to institute oneself *preliminarily*. All the more clearly it then emerged that this constitution was a provisional ruling. It had the advantage of leaving an open track to all the possi-

---

[constitutional state] (liberal counter-concepts against the *Führer*-state [*Führerstaat*]), one must look, beyond this word of a great statesman spoken from the *political* standpoint, simultaneously to the indignation stemming from *moral* motivations of a great poet and man of the people like Jeremias *Gotthelf*, who regards the term and concept of the "rule-of-law state" [*Rechtsstaat*] as the cause of all legal error of the nineteenth century; cf. on this my lecture at the Cologne Gautag of the Union of National Socialist German Jurists of 17 February 1934 printed in the *Juristischen Wochenschrift* 1934, p. 713ff. and *Deutsche Verwaltung* [*German Administration*], 1934, p. 35ff. [Schmitt here refers to: *Nationalsozialismus und Rechtsstaat*, pp. 713–718/pp. 35–42 of the mentioned journals.]

bilities of growth. But all the unholiness arising out of liberal constitutional statehood also had an open track. Everyone will understand that under the impression of an overwhelming, but swiftly passing National Liberal majority in the Reichstag, one could deceive oneself about this. Yet this does not release us from the obligation of seeing without prejudice the contradictions within the state composition of the new *Reich* nor does this release us from the obligation to scientifically evaluate the constitutional historical experiences.

4.

Bismarck says with good right, the King had only to make peace with the liberal Landtag opposition, not with the people, because the peace with the people was never interrupted. The representative system of a liberal constitutional state is however wholly laid out to create for the parliamentary "popular representative" the monopoly of the popular will and to hinder any other leadership [*Führung*] or immediate relation to the people as unconstitutional. Bourgeois civil constitutionalism did away with the leading [*Führung*] of the people via their King and supreme commander [*Oberster Kriegherr*], the cohesion of the Prussian King with his people, and subjected the German people to open or camouflaged direction via a human type, which was typologically ordered toward bourgeois civil constitutional thought, rather than toward the Prussian soldier state. Via this constitution, every authentic immediate appeal of the government to the people was made impossible. All new elections after the dissolution of the Reichstag (1887, 1893, 1906) showed that the majority of the German people was constantly ready to enter on the side of the German soldier state. But the system of a parliamentary party dominance mediated the political will of the people; it hindered the political working out of the popular will and placed a multiplicity of well-organized parties like a fixed wall between the political will of the government and the will of this people precisely rent apart and parceled out by parties. The Kaiser and King was constitutionally the "military" in contradistinction to the "political" *Führer*. Bourgeois civil rule-of-law constitutional state thought compelled everyone who wanted to be constitutionally correct to such fatal rendings of the economic against the political and of the political against the military which cleft the totality of the political.

A soldierly people was being cleft internally within a state composition dually assembled out of Prussian soldier state and bourgeois constitutional state. The army was in increasing measure spiritually isolated and a "state within the state." In this situation it had to *renounce*, beyond its own frame, raising the *total claim to leadership* [*totalen Führungsanspruch*] over the whole German people, a claim which pertains to each political *Führung* and decision. The general military duty seemingly stood and the army still seemed to be "the great educational school of the nation." But the concept of education of German bourgeois civil society was other than that of the Prussian soldier state. In the open collision of these "educational" claims the army modestly retreated. Via the institution of the single voluntary service year, bourgeois civil possession and bourgeois civil education – although they had changed essentially since the Wars of Liberation of 1813 – were also recognized by the military. What was decisive was that the army wished to be and ought to be the educational school of the nation *only for war*, and war appeared to the thought of this century as a rare case, as an extreme and isolated, swiftly resolved occasion. Most specialists, the generally dominant notion and voice reckoned with a war duration of half a year up to one year at most. To no avail, *Moltke* warned in a sitting of the Reichstag on 14 May 1890: "When the war which has now for more than ten years wafted over our heads like a sword of Damocles, – when this war breaks out, its duration and its end are not to be foreseen . . . It could be a seven years' war, it could be a thirty years' war." But the "dogma" of the brief duration of war with all the "specialists" was already imperturbable on economic and financial grounds.[13] The claim of the army to be an "educational school" and the claim to training and leadership [*Führungsanspruch*] following from it, related themselves, as an exceptional officer strikingly remarked, regrettably only to an *ultima ratio*,[xvii] to an exceptional, extreme special case, perceived to be abnormal, not an education encompassing the complete real life of the German people or exceeding in any sense the narrowest disciplinary frames of the military. "The preparation for *battle* is the main task of military training."[14] From decade to decade, one habituated oneself almost unconsciously ever more to the view that the army was a technical matter for itself, precisely that "foreign body," only stepping into action and quickly passing away for the most extreme case. The army withdrew into itself and was already on this basis in relation to the totality of the

---

[13] Reichsarchiv, *Der Weltkrieg 1914 bis 1918. Kriegsrüstung und Kriegswirtschaft*, Bd. I (Berlin, 1930), p. 333/34.

[14] Compare Moltke's memorandum of 25 July 1868 and the secret "Instruktion für die höheren Truppenführer" ["Instruction for the Higher Troop Leaders"] based upon it of 24 June 1869 (Moltke, *Taktisch-strategische Aufsätze*, p. 67; Curt Jany, *Geschichte der Königlich Preußischen Armee*, Vol. 4, 1933, p. 257).

German people spiritually in an almost fraught defensive position.

The German bourgeois intelligentsia of the pre-War period "couldn't swear an oath to the spirit of the nation."[15] The military leadership stood wholly in the spiritual defensive. Yet the complete state construction of the *Reich* made this bad situation almost hopeless after Bismarck's dismissal. Thus a great people of unheard of soldierly force, with an incomparable army and a technically perfected industrial apparatus, was drawn politically *Führer*-less into a World War.

5.

After Bismarck's dismissal, the German *Reich* had not only no political leadership [*Führung*], but no longer even that which one in the full sense can call a government. The inner-Prussian cleft between soldier state and bourgeois civil constitutionalism was not overcome or even mollified via the construction of a likewise "constitutional" *Reich*. Rather, the inner problematic of Prussia spread over the *Reich*. Thereby it became yet more complex, yet more expansive and deepened. The term "constitutional monarchy" and the misleading intonation placed upon the merely relative distinction between constitutional and parliamentary government veiled the inner contradictions of a bourgeois-legitimist compromise which leaves open the fundamental question, princely or popular sovereignty, dynastic or democratic principle? The

---

[15] Albrecht Erich *Günther* in the article "Die Intelligenz und der Krieg" [*The Intelligentsia and the War*] (in Ernst Jünger's collection "Krieg und Krieger" [*War and Warriors*] (Berlin, 1930), p. 95).

term "federal state" ["*Bundesstaat*"] covers over the inner contradiction between princely league and national unity state.

The state composition built itself upon the double soil of both these undecided questions. The fundamental political decisions were delayed. In consequence, a government was thereby only possible when one either, under cautious avoidance of the basic questions, held oneself to the narrow field of play of neutral occasions, or, rather, when a great statesman constantly balanced the counterpoised forces and played them out against one another. Bismarck achieved this for a while. With regard to the danger, which threatened German unity via the particularism of the German dynasties, Bismarck hoped that he could support himself upon a nationally reliable Reichstag elected by the whole German people, thus to stand upon the national state democratic soil; with regard to the powers of a pluralistic party system mainly organized into political Center Catholicism and Social Democracy and an unreliable Reichstag ruled by them, Bismarck could retreat to the "federal basis" of this Second *Reich*, and, if necessary, also into the Prussian state. The dynastic solidarity of the federal princes, the stately force of Prussia and the national homogeneity of the German people were, in this way, placed in the service of the political unity of Germany.

The advantage of this double and even threefold construction lay in that the one danger could be evoked against the other. The master of the foreign policy "game with the three spheres" and of "reinsurance" also knew how to hold this inner political ballgame in his hand. Admittedly, Bismarck's unexampled superiority pertains to this. Any other would have been smothered by the terrible weight of the political forces to be held in hand, and what with the great diplomats

was the highest ingenuity, would have had to metamor-
phose into puny tactics in the hands of lesser humans. But
after several years even Bismarck, as the National Liberal
Reichstag majority melted away, could no longer give secure
political leadership [*politische Führung*] to this state composition. He recognized that fundamental alterations were necessary. How far his plans for a coup d'état [*Staatsstreichpläne*]
really developed, is a question for itself.[16] However, that
with a man like Bismarck around the year 1890 the mere
thought, the mere consideration, could arise of dissolving
the Second *Reich* via the unanimous resolution of the federal
princes and founding it anew with a new constitution, shows
the deep exasperation, indeed, hopelessness, of this political
construct. In the moment, in which one no longer subjected
oneself to the political leadership [*Führung*] of one man,
any leadership and even any authentic government at all
fell away and there arose a destructive inner state confusion,
because the *Reich* as stately construction was preliminarily
only a regime, not yet an institution and the state composition contained no fixed constitutional order within itself.

[16] Egmont Zechlin, *Staatsstreichpläne Bismarcks und Wilhelms II. 1890–
1894* (Stuttgart, 1929), on this my article in the *Deutsche Allgemeine
Zeitung* of 10 July 1929 and the review by H. Rothfels in the *Deutsche
Literaturzeitung* 1929, pp. 2304–2316. In this article of 10 July 1929
one finds literally the following proposition: "Till now one does not yet
speak in Germany of pluralism and of the problem marked with this
word. It is apparently the misfortune not only of the kings, but of all
governing groups, that they feel the treatment of fundamental questions
to be unpleasant and rather hold themselves to the profit and applause
of daily politics. An authentic constitutional theory stands today before
a thankless task no less than in the era of Wilhelm II. On this there is
no lack of formalistic veiling and watering down."

One had indeed a liberal "construction," but no government and thus also in truth no constitution.

Who then could, if things were really to proceed with "constitutional correctness," govern at all in such a many-tracked system and really define the directions of policy? The "constitutional" German Kaiser and King of Prussia; the "responsible" *Reich*'s Chancellor; the Reichstag making use of its budgetary right; the purportedly sovereign Federal Council; the state governments; the Landtags of the individual states presiding over the most important sources of taxation? Or the authentically political force, the German soldier state and the military posts bearing it up, the supreme commander [*Oberste Kriegsherr*] with his counseling organs, Great General Staff and Civil Cabinet, or, standing between the soldier state and bourgeois civil constitutional state, the "responsible" Minister of War? Each could, from out of its responsibility or its well-grounded right of influence, by force of the totality of every authentically political question, claim the decision for itself. Each was compelled to play the one position off against the other, in order to enact that which it held to be correct. Each could object to the other that it was a "shadow government." One can say without exaggeration that such a state composition knows no government, but only shadow governments. Perhaps this condition would have grown aright of itself in a long undisturbed "organic" development. But the foreign policy and inner situation of Germany made this impossible and pressed toward a clear decision. The *Reich* and its government, Kaiser, *Reich*'s Chancellor and State Secretaries of the *Reich* Offices, grew gradually, beyond the delimitable division of competences, also with regard to Prussia into a leading position. In distinction to Wilhelm I, the Kaiser Wilhelm II already appeared more as German Kaiser than as Prussian King. But this development would have required greater spaces of time and more enduring happy successes in order to yield a result politically more secure. In the critical years before the outbreak of the World War the situation in state law was such that *Prussia no longer* and *the Reich did not yet lead*, while in terms of state law nothing had changed in the double and threefold construction of the federalistic *Bundesstaat*, Prussian hegemony and national unity state. In terms of state law, Germany had four armies and four ministers of war. The Prussian Minister of War actually exercised the functions of a *Reich* Minister of War; he was responsible for army bills and the army budget and even presented them before the Reichstag; but one had thereby to serve the internally contradictory and untrue fiction in state law that the Prussian Minister of War only appeared as Prussian plenipotentiary of the Federal Council in the Reichstag. The requisite means for the remaining armies, in any case, flowed from accounts of the *Reich*. On the basis of its budgetary right, recognized as holy, the Reichstag approved the means for the army. But, with the basic principles of the financial settlement of the time recognized in state law, the Reichstag had only indirect taxes at its disposal, while the direct taxes, in particular the income tax, remained with the states (*Länder*), whose armies were financially supported by the *Reich*. Attempts at direct *Reich* taxes, like the Inheritance Tax of 1906 and the one-off Defense Contribution of 1913, did not go anywhere. A *Reich* Income Tax was neither introduced via the inspiration of the first year, nor via the necessity of the last year of the War.

The Kaiser and King was supreme commander [*Oberster Kriegsherr*] and *Führer* of his army, which, by force of the oath of allegiance rendered unto him, was his followership, and conducted its discipline and honor without the countersignature of the Minister of War by force of his supreme command [*Kommandogewalt*]. But this Kaiser and *Führer* was simultaneously a constitutional monarch; he was, according to the recognized principles of the constitutional system, not responsible and his orders required, in order to be binding, the countersignature of the *Reich*'s Chancellor, or of a minister, who "thereby assumed responsibility." Even the distinction between constitutional and parliamentary monarchy cannot make out of the nonresponsible monarch those positions which really governed with constitutional correctness. It is not thinkable that a valid, written constitution expressly fixes a responsibility and then one Other[xviii] than the one responsible leads and governs. Herewith it is wholly equipollent how the responsibility of the Nearer[xix] one is led through and organized, whether it is realized in the forms of justice, or parliamentarily via votes of no confidence, or plebiscitarily via popular referenda. The constitutional fixing of responsibility is decisive and as mere basic principle in the long run also politically strong enough in order somehow to create the procedure of its responsibility so long as some constitutionally recognized political force has the word of the constitution on its side. That a responsible minister with a statutory proposal or with a budgetary question must stand before a parliament for questioning and response, suffices to grant political reality to the responsibility of the minister and to the nonresponsibility of the constitutional monarch. This can be more effective and more consequential than all constitutional statutorily normed duties for dismissal by a parliamentary motion of no confidence. The linkage of such a fundamental constitutional ministerial responsibility with the budgetary right of the parliament doubly sanctioned via the Indemnity of 1866 thus hindered the monarch and his ministers from really being able to govern. On the other hand, however, there was also no parliamentary government. The far-famed system of a constitutional (in distinction to a parliamentary) monarchy is thus set up, in a state of the type of the Second *Reich*, to destroy any normal possibility of an authentic government. It required the extraordinary force and adroitness of a Bismarck in order to make valid the responsibility before the Reichstag to the King and other positions, and to make valid the responsibility before the Kaiser and King to the Reichstag and via such a back and forth to create a space of play for his leadership. But even this was only possible, as was already mentioned, as long as the effect of his astounding successes of 1866 and 1871 and the National Liberal parliamentary majority held out. The grounding of the Petition of Release of 18 March 1890 shows clearly enough how strongly the constitutional responsibility presses the *Reich*'s Chancellor or Minister President on the side of the parliament and, as Bismarck said, "builds the essence of constitutional life."[17]

The supreme commander accordingly had, beyond his military supreme command [*Kommandogewalt*] only a *potestas indirecta*,[xx] and, as the Military and the Political were

---

[17] Bismarck's Petition calls up the claim that the Cabinet Order of 8 September 1852 only gives to the Minister President (and to the Minister of War), not to every minister of state, the competence to hold forth immediately before the King. "In the absolute monarchy, it was a dispensable stipulation, as contained in the Ordre of 1852, and would still be today, if we recurred to Absolutism, without ministerial responsibility. According to the constitutional institutions persisting in the law, however, a ministerial presiding over the leading of the Collegium of Ministers on the basis of 1852 is indispensable."

conceptually ripped asunder, no authentic possibility of government. He was not responsible; precisely for that reason the proposition also held for him: *le roi règne et ne gouverne pas.*[xxi] Wilhelm I understood that. The later attempts toward a "personal rule" altered nothing essential in this and only had illusionary prestige effects. In every constitutional order,[xxii] the position of a monarch is hardly construable at all, and *Lorenz von Stein*, the one best acquainted, claims that no human cleverness suffices to resolve the internal contradictions of the position of a constitutional head of state. According to the situation of the matter, such unclarities have some political advantages, but also great disadvantages. In any case, they compel the constitutional King, who himself desires to define the directions of policy and take the essential political decisions, finally before the simple dilemma of either exercising his influence in an inconspicuous way indirectly, or, however, to lay aside the constitutional responsibility of his ministers. It is an error in constitutional questions to desire to distinguish between juristic and political. The contradictory double role of a correct constitutional monarch, i.e. a monarch not responsible as a consequence of the countersignature of a responsible minister and of a monarch as sole highest *Führer* of the army bound to no ministerial countersignature, and thus exempted from any constitutional responsibility, only repeats the above represented inner contradiction and cleft between bourgeois civil constitutional state and Prussian soldier state.

The *Reich*'s Chancellor, by contrast, was constitutionally responsible, but simultaneously dependent upon the trust of his constitutionally nonresponsible kaiserly Lord and, beyond this, as Prussian Minister President member of a Collegium, which he did not hold securely in his hand. Every parliamentary consideration of an army bill showed that the

Reich's Chancellor and Prussian Minister President, despite all distinctions, was also really responsible to the parliament and that the inner logic of bourgeois constitutionalism leads to parliamentarism. This is, when the budgetary right of the parliament stands beyond doubt, a question of time, of means and ways, but not of the final result. With help of a recognized budgetary right every parliament can seize the political leadership for itself, and thus hinder it for any other. Indeed, the political is the total and this totality allows itself to be enacted just as well and just as logically from the economic and financial side as from the military side.

In this constitutional situation, the Reichstag self-evidently strived to hold the strength of the German army in dependence upon the approval of the annual budget. With this striving, the Reichstag had political success. In any event, the constitution clearly and distinctly prescribed the general military duty: "Every German owes military service and cannot allow himself to be represented in the exercise of this duty" (Article 57). But while in other cases the holiness of the constitution and of every constitutional word was proclaimed with all invocations of a rule-of-law- and constitutional state ideology, one self-evidently passed over this word of the constitution, because here, as long as the army was not a parliamentary army, it concerned the soldier state component of the state composition. In the collision between the enactment of the general military duty and the power claims of budgetary right of the parliament, the consideration of the parliament was victorious. The strength of the peacetime presence of the German army was normed in Article 60 of the *Reich* Constitution of 1867 to one person per hundred of the population (401,659), first only until 31 December 1871, then prolonged via *Reich* statute to 1874. For later times it was to be fixed by way of *Reich* legislation, i.e. via new compromises with the Reichstag. As in a decisive political question of this type an annual dependence upon the changing parliamentary majority was manifestly senseless, here, too, it came down to typical, compromising intermediate solutions, to agreements for seven or latterly for five or six years, to septennials, sexennials, quinquennials,[18] which, however had to be interrupted via supernumerary, extraordinary, unscheduled proposals and renewals in ascending measure, because the situation constantly changed, and, as the World War approached, the military preparation of Germany no longer kept pace with the armament of its neighbors. The political right of decision of the Reichstag thereby became ever stronger and the logic of the constitutional development toward parliamentarism stepped ever more clearly into broad daylight.

With danger growing, the reports of the Great General Staff to the Minister of War became from year to year more urgent. They are today documents of an internally impossible constitutional condition clefting a great *Reich* from within. Proposals of the General Staff, whose political reason everyone recognizes today, invocations, whose force and grandeur shakes anyone capable of freeing themselves from the sophistry of bourgeois civil constitutionalism, warnings, whose political farsightedness everyone must admire, remained without effect. They had, immediately before a terrible war,

---

[18] 1st Septennial 1881–88; 2nd Septennial 1887–94; 1st Quinquennial 1894–99; 2nd Quinquennial 1899–1904, extended to 31 March 1905; Sexennial of 1905–1911; 3rd Quinquennial from 1911–1916. During this last Quinquennial the World War of 1914 broke out; via the army preparations of 1912 and 1913 unplanned-for alterations were undertaken, without anything being altered in the basic law of the quinquennial system.

with which everyone had to reckon, to fail ever and again on the inner contradictions of the stately organization, so that today everyone can claim that nobody took any responsibility. The German General Staff displayed itself in the life-question of the German people, in the question of the preparation for a total war, as the true bearer of all political *Führer*-qualities of the German people. But the logic of bourgeois civil constitutionalism stood in the way of every state political and folkish logic [*völkischen Logik*]. It broke from within the state composition of the German *Reich*, in that it pressed the soldier state into a constitutionally abnormal situation. It repeated in the course of an externally splendid half century, inconspicuously and unconsciously, but now with resounding success, the same comportment, which in the conflictual period before the year 1866 attempted to hinder with loud oppositional noise the real preparation for the war, at that time without success. In vain, the General Staff appealed to the fact that the essence of the general military duty prescribed by the constitution does not consist in the one percent but rather in that those ready at hand and fit for service be trained. The general military duty could not really be implemented because implementing this would have endangered the budgetary right of the Reichstag and therewith bourgeois civil constitutionalism itself, and this endangerment, in turn, would have called for internal and foreign policy restrictions and reservations. Even the attempt to introduce a control over the *Landsturm*,[xxiii] as this existed in France and Russia, in Germany as well, failed on such restrictions.[19] The political result of this condition was

[19] Reichsarchiv, *Der Weltkrieg 1914 bis 1918. Kriegsrüstung und Kriegswirtschaft*, Bd. I (Berlin, 1930), p. 51.

summed up in a protocol from the year 1905 by the Chief of the General Staff, Generaloberst *von Schlieffen*, shortly before his exit: "We invented the general military duty and the people in arms and demonstrated the necessity of introducing these institutions to other nations. After we brought our sworn enemies to augment their armies immeasurably, we left off our exertions. We still poke about at our number of inhabitants, at the masses of the population, which stand as a commandment for us, but these masses are not trained and armed in the full number of those needed."[20]

As the danger of this first clearly rose to consciousness and Minister of War *von Verdy* in the year 1890 seriously drafted the plan to implement the general military duty, the Reichstag gave a fundamental answer in four resolutions of its budgetary commission on 16 June 1890, which the Reichstag adopted on 28 June 1890, with a great majority. One must historically link up these resolutions into a line with the Peace Resolution of the Reichstag of 19 July 1917 drawn up during the World War, in order to recognize the deeper contexts of the "constitution" of such a *Reich*. In those resolutions of 1890, the expectation is articulated in all sharpness "that the federated governments shall stand back from the following of plans through which all war-capable men should be led to active service, in which thereby precisely unsustainable costs would arise for the German Reich."[21] The further demands of these resolutions concerned the abolition of the period defined for the septennial and the state-year as period of approval, the diminution of the actual time of presence with the active army and finally

---

[20] *Op. cit.*, p. 86.
[21] *Op. cit.*, Anlagenband I, p. 45.

the introduction of the statutory two-year service period for foot soldiers. This was actually already implemented in the year 1892. In the course of the following years, from bill to bill, in increasing measure, it then emerged that the "purely budgetary" restrictions not only further increased the inner and foreign policy hindrances but also, above all, it emerged that the political positions of the *Reich*, *Reich*'s Chancellor, State Secretary of the Interior, State Secretary of the *Reich* Treasury Office *inter alia*, even the Prussian Minister of War, had to become *organs of the inner state conflict*.

The state composition of the Second *Reich* was namely of the kind such that all the doubts of the different departments against the most necessary military defense of Germany drew upon the inner state opposition of inimical political forces and tendencies. Not only the general opposition between military and civil, also the deeper conflict between bourgeois civil constitutionalism and Prussian soldier state, between national democratic unity state and dynastic federal state, worked their way into the organizational composition of the *Reich* and clefted its unified political will from within. The cleaving and juxtaposition of political and military, political and economic thereby was elevated, so to speak, into a constitutional institution. Political leadership was only possible as a passing apparent consequence of victorious wars and happy successes, not however on the basis of the foundation of a secure state composition and as fixed presupposition for the material preparation of a dangerous World War. Today it is possible to recognize that the preparation for a measure, which *Ernst Jünger* has labeled as "total mobilization," likewise must be total. In the pre-War period as well, knowledge or at least the inkling of this necessity was in no way lacking. Under the impression of the Balkan War of

1912, all positions coming into consideration attained the conviction that at least for the nourishment of the German people in the war economic measures would have to be prepared. At the first council meeting sitting on 21 December 1912 there took part: representatives of the *Reich* Office of the Interior, of the Foreign Office, of the *Reich* Treasury Office, of the *Reich* Naval Office, of the General Staff, of the Kaiserly Statistical Office, of the *Reich* Bank, of the Prussian Ministry of the Interior, of Agriculture, Domains and Forests, of Finances, of Public Work, of Trade, of the Ministry of War and of the Prussian Statistical Land Office. The complexity of the bureaucratic apparatus was thus great enough. It also came to the building of commissions and sub-commissions, yet a real success did not emerge. Here, too, it's not a matter of fixing personal guilt, but rather of recognizing the organizational system of a state composition in which every difference between the different departments immediately had to be drawn into the inner state cleft between inimical tendencies. The natural order of a real state essence was thereby disturbed in that different offices had to draw up their resolutions not only in view of the natural opposition with other departments, but also in *pre-emption of the viewpoints of the internal political enemy.*

What this means is shown by a typical expression of the Prussian Minister of War von Einem, which is addressed to the *Reich*'s Chancellor von Bülow in June of 1906: "The General Staff and the transport troops say from the military standpoint that it's not a matter of costs, which also takes alterations into account, and which lie far from the political concerns: 'as fast as possible, immediately.' For me, however, it's not done with such a simple solution of the question. I must regard it from the political and financial standpoint and beyond that *take into consideration that the regard for the military administration can only profit, the less it has to alter its views before the legislative factors* ... Whether we can wait so long (up to the end of the quinquennial at that time), is *solely a political question*; militarily we can help ourselves with *improvisations*. It's illuminating that the quinquennial binds our hands in some relations. Shall we give it up on that account? I do not believe that this would be to the purpose, as then with every further configuration of the army the embittered and targeted agitations against the existence of the army which come out would be all the more dangerous with their annual return."[22]

This expression of a good Prussian officer is a vivid example of the counter-purposive rending asunder of the political and the military and of the relocation of internal political restrictions within the shared work of state departments. It is simultaneously an example that in such a state construction the *Prussian Minister of War* had to become *the authentically tragic figure*. If one has said with right of constitutional monarchs that no human cleverness suffices to rightly construe their position, then one must say of the Prussian Minister of War of the Second *Reich* that his position was nearly monstrous and absurd. The King could always by force of his personal irresponsibility assume political influence from out of an invisible position. The Chief of the General Staff did not need to tread upon the inner political battleground and did not need to appear before the Reichstag. By contrast, the Minister of War stood in the intersection of all inner state battlelines of a so difficultly organized *Reich*. The battle was fought out upon his spine;

---

[22] *Op. cit.*, Anlagenband I, p. 101/2.

his occupational domain was pulverized from all sides. He was as Prussian state minister a member of the Collegium led by the Prussian Minister President, but did not have according to the Cabinet Order of 8 September 1852 the competence of immediately holding forth with the King. He was responsible before the Reichstag, although it, as mentioned, essentially did not depend how this responsibility was construed in constitutional law; that he is "responsible," that he must stand before the parliament insisting on its budgetary right and submit to question and answer, suffices in order to give the responsibility its political and state legal reality. Yet he is self-evidently also always Prussian soldier and officer, the military subordinate of his Highest Commander, Warlord and Judge, before whom he immediately holds forth. He thus also always needs as well the trust of his kingly sponsor, from whom, however, he takes over the responsibility via his countersignature, who thus, because wholly irresponsible, cannot himself confer a constitutionally substantial trust. This contradictory, internally impossible position now becomes confined via the exemption of the supreme command [*Kommandogewalt*] out of the constitutional system to mere military administration, in contradistinction to the supreme command. Just as little as the opposition between Prussian soldier state and bourgeois constitutional state is a mere "separation of powers," is the distinction between supreme command and military administration in such a constitutional situation an issue of mere administrative expedience or even reason. It becomes a principled question of state and constitutional law of the first rank, which touches upon the last political roots of the whole essence of the state. Bismarck articulated this in his Reichstag speech of 11 January 1887. The consequence is that the occupational domain of the Minister of War, which in such a way is restricted to military administration, becomes cut off from the essential core of the military, from the supreme command, and with help from the antithesis between military and civil is pressed to the side of the "civil," with help from the antithesis between military and political is pressed to the side of the "political." Every success, which the Prussian soldier state wrested from liberal constitutionalism, that it knew to exempt the supreme command from the system of the bourgeois civil constitutional state, worked itself out departmentally *against* the Prussian Minister of War. To the cost of his occupational domain the tasks of leading the army and essential personnel issues like the naming of officers were transferred to other positions, to the General Staff and Military Cabinet. These thereby fell into a natural and ineluctable rivalry with the Minister of War, who had to fight for his department on all sides, against the parliament and the army, against the General Staff and the Military Cabinet, although, as shown above, the deep internal political oppositions of a clefted state construction drove themselves into the opposed viewpoints of the different departments like a wedge.

With Roon as the Minister of War this did not emerge so conspicuously, because Roon had fought through the conflict with the Landtag alongside the King and Bismarck. The great common work of the army reform and of the common, all-ruling, opposition against the parliament, during an open conflict, gripped all co-workers of Wilhelm I, relativized their mutual differences and rivalries and made possible for this time of an abnormal constitutional situation a normal enactment of the soldierly component of this state composition. This was altered after the Wars of 1871, as an externally normal complete situation emerged. On 1 January 1873, there arose the curious condition that Prussia, and mediately the *Reich* as well, for almost a year had two Ministers of War at the same time. Roon became Prussian Minister President, but remained Minister of War and in this capacity Chair of the Commission of the Federal Council [*Bundesrat*] for the Land Army and the Forts; Lieutenant General von Kameke, who became State Minister and Member of the Prussian State Ministry, led the activities of a "second Chief of the Army Administration" and, indeed, "with full effect" in the manner that recourse against his decisions did not somehow go to Roon, but rather immediately to the King. Bismarck officially ignored this second Minister of War; he also energetically hindered the attempts of Roon and Kameke to make the Prussian Minister of War into "an organ of the Kaiser."[23] After Roon's departure, after General von Kameke was named sole Prussian Minister of War on 9 November 1873, he soon found himself in enduring and forlorn frictions with both the Chief of the Military Cabinet von Albedyll as well as with the General Quartermaster Count Waldersee. The ten years of his activity as Minister of War were filled full with internal conflicts on the content

[23] Otto Küsel-Glogau, "Bismarck. Beiträge zur inneren Politik" [Bismarck. Contributions to domestic policy], with a foreword by the Reichsminister of Finance Graf Schwerin von Krosigk (Berlin, 1934), p. 53f. This book contains particularly disclosive proofs for how any question, however "purely financial," i.e. the merciful competence over a sum from a disposable fund, can become a highly political question. When on pp. 95–97 Bismarck's grounds against the proposals of Roon and Kameke are treated as untenable, then it appears to me to mistake both the authentic difficulty of Bismarck's situation as well as the problematic of the Reich's composition.

and scope of his department, although he finally stood confronted with a common front of the Military Cabinet, General Staff and *Reich*'s Chancellor. When he finally bid farewell to the Ministry of War, in March 1883, this old Prussian soldier gave out the maxim: "With me, the last Prussian Minister of War departs from this house."[24]

[24] Rudolf Schmidt-Bückeburg, *Das Militärkabinett der preußischen Könige und deutschen Kaiser* (Berlin, 1933), p. 151.

II. THE COLLAPSE

In the year 1866, decisive for the following half-century, the Prussian soldier state had the swift military victory and foreign policy success, the liberal movement, however, had the "constitution" on its side. Upon this foundation the delay of the conflict arose, but not any state composition ordered in itself. What had to step in, when victory and success were lacking?

1.

With military victories and foreign policy successes like those of 1866 and 1870, any liberal bourgeois citizenry can reconcile itself well with army and war. But to this pertains precisely a victorious army and a war leading to economic prosperity. Without this, the Landtag would not have spoken of indemnity but of a breach of the constitution and of [appeal to the] *Staatsgerichtshof.* War is also in no way generally and unconditionally rejected even by the most liberal bourgeoisie; a victorious war can even be held by the bourgeoisie to be a "social ideal," but naturally only a *victorious* war. However, no state, and least of all a state of the structure of Prussia, can allow itself seriously to go in for such claims and "ideals"; no institution, and least of all the political unity of a people, can institute itself upon the fortunate case and make its type of existence dependent upon uninterrupted lucky successes. If the luck once lapsed, if the war once ceased to be successful, then the fundamental presupposition of the "constitutional compromise" would fall away. Then the liberal opposition of 1866 would have been right. The bourgeois citizen must have felt himself to be deceived and demanded the consequentially liberal democratic constitutional state as his good right. Herewith it is wholly equipollent as to whether the individual liberals qua individuals were well-meaning patriotic and educated people or not. They were certainly all good bourgeois citizens and only wished for the best. Yet they all stood under the law of their political movement, within the compulsion of the internal political complete structure of the Prussian state and of the Second *Reich* based upon it, which they themselves induced. The Prussian soldier state, however, politically subjected itself to the bourgeois civil claim to victorious wars and economic prosperity, when after the victorious war it bade for indemnity and received it. The law of the further inner state development of Prussia and of Germany was now in place.

As the inner oppositions of such a state had neither the foreign policy security nor temporal expanses at their disposal, which were necessary in order to create even the possibility of a balancing organic growth, for the Prussian soldier state there were only three thinkable continuations of this constitutional situation: either the clear revolutionary decision via the full inner political victory of one counterpart over the others, of the soldier over the bourgeois citizen or of the bourgeois citizen over the soldier; or a sinking of Germany down to a political level upon which all inner contradictions were irrelevant, because the whole political unity had become irrelevant, thus sinking down to the historical rank of a middling state borne up by extra-German league systems and the renunciation of German Great Power status and its historical mission; or finally, third, heroic decline in full consciousness of the lost position. Today, in the clearest consequentiality it can be recognized that for a soldier state of the Prussian type after a century of liberalism only the last possibility came into consideration. While the bourgeoisie since the year 1917 and namely in the Weimar constitution allowed itself to go in for a sad and posthumous type of fulfillment of its "constitutional claims," it was the glory of this soldier state and a warrant for the resurrection of Germany, that it went the heroic way.

The cleft of the inner state structure broke out during the World War and pulverized the force of resistance. Foreign descriptions of the rapport between war-leading and state-leading for the World War 1914–18 gladly proceed upon the assumption that the relation between military power and civil power, army brass and government, was in no way a serious problem for Germany during the war, because the Kaiser as supreme commander had an unrestricted power in a non-parliamentary governed state.[25] This is a superficial view, which is based upon an errant exaggeration of the distinction between constitutional and parliamentary monarchy. The exemption of the supreme command [*Kommandogewalt*] of the Kaiser from the bourgeois civil constitutional system even during the war remained a sign that the complete structure of the state was clefted and this cleft deepened itself with the augmenting expansion and intensity of the World War. Perhaps some friction could have been avoided via common counseling merged into a Highest War Council before the supreme commander. In all war-waging lands it came to critical oppositions between the army leadership and the government.[26] They are misleadingly treated under the

[25] Thus, for example: J.M. Bourget, *Gouvernement et Commandement* [Les Leçons de la Guerre Mondiale] (Paris: Payot, 1930).

[26] Cf. Fritz Hartung, *op. cit.*, p. 370; on the state law development in

general rubric of the opposition between "military and politics." In truth, it transpired that the totality of the war aim asserted itself in every war-waging land. This totality cannot be isolated, but rather is taken in claim out of every domain. Consequently, it expresses itself not only as the totality claim of war-waging but also as the totality claim of political state conduct and equally of economic conduct.[xxiv] The German constitutional situation was now of the type that the collisions and differences between army brass and government, between military and civil competence, emerging in all war-waging lands, in Germany always had to push toward their ground, namely toward the unresolved conflict between Prussian soldier state and bourgeois constitutional state and thus had to work themselves out in internal politics in a state and people destroying way. It is not a matter of whether the objection of "self-exclusion" is apt for the Kaiser; in the given constitutional situation he could hardly act otherwise than he acted.[27] But with constitutional correctness such a

---

France, which from 1914 to 1918 attempted four different systems, see the thoroughly instructive presentation of Esmein-Nézard, *Éléments de Droit Constitutionnel français et comparé*, Bd. 2, 7. Aufl. (Paris, 1921), p. 143f., and the articles by Barthélemy, *Le Droit public en temps de guerre; les pouvoirs publics et le commandement militaire*, in the *Revue du droit public*, 1916 and 1917.

[27] In the growing self-exclusion of the Kaiser, Colonel Schwertfeger (*Die politischen und militärischen Verantwortlichkeiten im Verlaufe der Offensive 1918; Gutachten für den parlamentarischen Untersuchungsausschuß über den deutschen Zusammenbruch 1918* (Berlin, 1927) sees the authentic cause of the opposition between government and army brass. On this the high archival counsel, W. Foerster, *Deutscher Offizier-Bund*, Bd. 4, Nr. 23f. says: "The constitutional system surely lays upon the monarch not merely a formal but also a moral responsibility, but it still allocates the brunt of the practical work in the preparation and carrying out

war could not be won for Germany, but rather only lost, as indeed the preparation for the war furthered in vain by the General Staff had already been lost.

The inner breach in the state composition of the Second *Reich*, which only concealed and delayed rather than overcame the opposition between Prussian soldier state and bourgeois civil constitutional state, stepped openly into broad daylight as the military situation became difficult. Every personal difference between the *Reich*'s Chancellor and an army leader [*Heerführer*] immediately touched upon the last roots of this inner-state dualism and ripped off the veil of seeming compromise of the constitutional system. The wars of 1864, 1866 and 1870 took a swift and victorious course, but despite this already allowed the thoroughly isolated, inner political defensive situation of the soldierly state core to be recognized. During the World War, every worsening of the military or foreign policy situation had, with almost mathematical exactitude, immediately to redound to the benefit of the counter-player, to the parliament, and to render unto it constitutional arguments for

---

of tasks to the co-responsible departments . . . In the last year of the World War, however, the military counsel of the monarch stood at the height of their task, but not, however, the political counsel." Lt. Col. A. Niemann, *Kaiser und Heer* (Berlin, 1929), pp. 367–368, claims the Kaiser bought the balance between the preponderance of the army brass and the political leadership [*Führung*] almost constantly with personal sacrifices of the most difficult type, in particular with inner political losses of prestige and the forces of the German people striving toward popular sovereignty exploited the cleft between the military and the political war leadership. This is apt; however, it first becomes recognizable out of the constitutional construction of the Second Reich in its authentic bearing.

new claims to power. Both component parts of the state composition detached themselves from one another and developed themselves, separated from one another, each according to its inner law under the irresistible compulsion of a fraught war. Only out of the complete state structure of the Second *Reich* does the fact explain itself which *Oncken*[28] captures: "Whilst the opposition of the departments in the year 1870–71 only slightly percolated beyond the circles privy to it, only occasionally found a light echo in the press, but to the people itself, the battlers as well as the homeland remained concealed, yet in the World War the opposition of the departments fell in ascending measure into the public sphere, into the press, into the parties, into the organizations . . . Therewith the problem of 'politics and war-waging' elongated itself, for the first time with such scope, into the soul of an entire people deeply agitated in its depths. . . ." The opposition could thus elongate and deepen itself, because it was concatenated and organized deeply in the constitutional situation. Instead of the internal political unitedness of the German people becoming stronger and more fortified with the growing danger, the logic of the constitutional dualism between soldier and bourgeois citizen, and in its succession then also the artificial opposition between soldier and (succeeding the bourgeois citizen) worker, acted in the opposite direction. Every disappointment, every difficulty of waging war gave retrospective justice to the arguments of the opposition of 1866 which had only been assuaged by a splendid success and ripped open anew the conflict which had been covered over only via a victorious war. The undischarged

---

[28] *Politik und Kriegführung*, Münchener Universitätsreden, Heft 12 (München, 1927), p. 28.

contradictions of the inner state complete composition, the conflict of the Prussian soldier state against a bourgeois civil constitutional state, the ill fact that the authentic constitutional compromise and therewith the state composition itself was only based upon a swiftly won, *victorious* war, all this in the compulsion of such a constitutional system with the growing difficulties of the situation of the World War turned into a fundamental, indeed, world-view and total opposition between government and people, and finally into the fatal opposition between army and homeland, soldier and worker. On this, Germany collapsed.

The refusal of the Army Loan became for the openly treasonous and country-betraying parties the legal, constitutionally correct point of incursion. The majority of the Reichstag wanted no betrayal, but indeed strengthening of the immunity for members of the Reichstag, thus expansion of the breach point for the treason, and consequently implementation of the parliamentary system, i.e. the constitutional ideal of the enemies. Still during the War, in the legal forms of Bismarck's constitution, the bourgeois civil constitutional state triumphed over the Prussian-German soldier state. After the famed Peace Resolution of 19 July 1917, with the negotiation of the budgetary plan for 1917/18, the Reichstag set up a "Constitutional Commission" which demanded a tighter regulation of the responsibility of the *Reich*'s Chancellor before the Reichstag and demanded the countersignature of the Minister of War or of the *Reich*'s Chancellor even for the naming of officers. The last Chancellors of the *Reich*, Count Hertling and Prince Max von Baden, were already parliamentary ministers. On 28 October 1918, there were enacted the constitutionally altering statutes of 28 October 1918, likewise legally and constitutionally correct, issued and announced by the Kaiser, which fulfilled all these demands of the parliament and culled the last remnants of the Prussian soldier state out of the constitution. They did not hold back the collapse, but they are meaningful as the logical conclusion of monarchic constitutionalism. *G. Anschütz*, the classic author of liberal state law doctrine, remarked upon this last legislative expression of the Second *Reich*: It "enacted the subordination of the military power under the civil power and laid aside a piece of 'militarism', which pertained to the particularities of the Prussian-German state law, and which indubitably stood in contradiction with the principles of the constitutional state, doing so by subjecting the entire war operation, and indeed not only the military administration, but rather also the army brass to ministerial responsibility and therewith to the influence of the Reichstag."

Indubitably. This was the voice of the putatively unpolitical, purely juristic state law doctrine. The army dissolved itself; the weapons were delivered over to the enemy. Bourgeois civil constitutionalism victoriously triumphed over the Prussian-German "militarism."

2.

The Prussian soldier state, courageous and victorious in the field, stood throughout a whole century spiritually in a fraught defensive, indeed in full defenselessness. Its political opponents ruled the language and concepts of the time. To their benefit alone redounded the great argument of the "impression in foreign countries." Victorious wars, stately achievements of unexampled grandeur were thereby brought to their historical reward in that one believed one had to weaken internal politically necessary decisions on account of considerations in foreign policy.

In three decisive moments in the history of the last century the spiritual subjection under the legal notion of the opponent defined in an unholy manner the destiny of Germany. First, apparently unimportant and apparently not decisive on 5 August 1866, when one believed one could afford it, to beseech the liberal opposition, with the superiority and generosity of the victor and in the moment of success, for indemnity and to accommodate oneself to its concepts of law and constitution without danger. The second moment lies at the beginning of the World War and opens the gigantic battle of the peoples with a terrible spiritual defeat for Germany. The German *Reich*'s Chancellor Bethmann Hollweg saw the spiritual justification of the German War in the "battle against Czarism"; the German people battling for its national existence was subordinated to the war aim and constitutional ideology of Western liberal democracy, which were simultaneously the political ideals of the internal political enemies of the Prussian soldier state. But the spiritual subjection under the legal concepts of the enemy went yet further. On 4 August 1914 the German *Reich*'s Chancellor in his speech to the Reichstag declared the march of the German army into Belgium to be an "injustice," which one would have to make right. A childish emergency jurisprudence bound up with a servile angst about the impression in foreign countries, led to this shameful capitulation and betrayed the German people's army to the constitutional ideals and legal concepts of its foreign and inner political enemies. The third moment finally fulfilled this development: in the statutes of 28 October 1918, the ideas of the liberal democratic constitutional state, still within the legality of Bismarck's constitution, triumphed over the spirit of the German people and effected the inner lack of resistance of the battling German army.

These three days – 5 August 1866, 4 August 1914 and 28 October 1918 – stand in a single mutually related line of development. The above-mentioned (p. 43)[xxv] Reichstag resolution of 28 June 1890 and the Peace Resolution of the Reichstag of 19 July 1917 remain wholly within the frame of the segments of German constitutional history defined by these three days. In their succession a law consequentially unfolds itself: first the inner political spiritual subjection of the Prussian soldier state under the legal concepts of the bourgeois civil rule-of-law and constitutional state; then the subjection under the spiritual war aim of the enemy, bound up with the subaltern striving of making a good impression in foreign countries and of appeasing the enemy via spiritual yielding and "objectivity"; and finally the open renunciation of the Prussian soldier state and the constitutionally sanctioned subjection under the state and legal ideals of a precisely thereby victorious, merciless enemy. The logic of spiritual subordination fulfills itself in resistanceless political servitude.

3.

If the constitutional claims of the liberal bourgeois citizenry in Germany had been justified, and if they corresponded in any authentic sense with the real German complete constitution, then they would now have had opportunity to overcome the cleft and to mediate the closed political unity of state, army, people and economy. The party leaders [*Parteiführer*] and professional politicians of the parliamentary "opposition" heretofore were now compelled to demonstrate the justification of their battle against the Prussian soldier state with a political achievement, instead of with speeches against unconstitutional militarism, to demonstrate their right to lead [*Führerrecht*] and, instead of making their normativistic arguments valid with cheap right-havery [*Rechthaberei*] under the protection of the courageous soldier state, with their concretely realized constitutional ideal itself to stand the test within the crucible of political danger.

In fact, one can only understand the Weimar constitution of 1919, as it exists, as an answer to the half-century questions of the conflicts relating to the Prussian-German army and constitution. I would not regard it as an "intermediate constitution," as my esteemed colleague *G.A. Walz* does.[29] With the collapse of the Prussian soldier state, the Weimar constitution is, as a state construction, only the shadowy, surviving for a short time, bourgeois civil part of the clefted state composition of the collapsed *Reich*. When this constitution in Article 25, paragraph 2 specifies that the President of the *Reich* can only dissolve the Reichstag once for the same cause, then this is consciously and expressly the answer to the repeated dissolutions of the Prussian Landtag during the conflict years 1862–1866. When in Article 50 it is said that all orders and mandates upon the domain of the military [*Wehrmacht*] are in need of countersignature, then this is the fulfillment of a demand, which the liberal bourgeoisie had raised for a half-century and decides the half-century battle concerning the supreme command of the King apparently in favor of the parliament. And when in

---

[29] G.A. Walz, *Das Ende der Zwischenverfassung* (Stuttgart: Verlag von W. Kohlhammer, 1933).

Article 176 it is prescribed that all members of the military [*Wehrmacht*] are "to be sworn by oath to this constitution," then this is the retrospective gratification for the fact that the Prussian oath of allegiance for soldiers was sworn to the lords of the land and not to the constitution. French royalists have often defined the republic as the mere "absence of the King," "*l'absence du roi*."[xxvi] Of this Weimar constitution, one must say that it wasn't even that. It was only the delayed confrontation with the no longer present Prussian soldier state, the other component part of the bipartite state composition, which after the falling away of its counter-element unrolled itself without restraint. The Weimar constitution gave an answer to a question that had fallen away, which was no longer really posed in the present. The victory of liberal democracy, which announced itself in the Weimar constitution, was only posthumous. It was directed toward the past, without present and without future, unreal, the victory which a specter bears away over the shade of his opponent.

That in the year 1919 one held such constitutional announcements and documentations to be necessary shows how much the state constructive problematic for the state consciousness of the German people was still defined by the internal political situation of the nineteenth century. No new state thought was inclined to fill in the vacuum which emerged from the falling away of the military monarchy. The federal state structure of the *Reich* was helplessly retained, but the hegemony of Prussia was energetically set aside, so that the "errant construction" of a neither hegemonic nor equally balanced federal state construction emerged. In a "Second Main Part" of the Weimar constitution, under the superscript "Basic Rights and Basic Duties of the Germans," an inter-fraction party program is appended to the organizational first Main Part, which was based upon a well-meaning attempt by Friedrich Naumann, but which could give no substance to the constitution. It contained, next to and inter-mixed with one another, liberal democratic, social democratic and Catholic Center principles, which were without mutual relation and also without organizational connection with the first Main Part of the Constitution. A connection existed only to the extent that as dilatory formal compromises between three contradictory, mutually dissolving world-views, as well as the value-neutral and truth-neutral first Main Part, in their practical result had to lead to an empty, parity-based neutrality. Article 148 of this Constitution is a loyal expres-sion of such a nothing but neutral state. "With instruction in public schools care is to be taken that the sentiments of those thinking otherwise [*Andersdenkender*] are not wounded." The State Court for the German *Reich* interpreted this sentence in its decision of 11 July 1930 on the question of Thuringian school prayer (*Decisions in Civil Matters* [*Entscheidungen in Zivilsachen*], vol. 129, Appendix p. 9f.) with a grounding which shall remain for all times a document of "neutral" thought and sentiment. It concerns the question of whether German children in German schools may pray to God in the school prayer that God may make us "free from deceit and betrayal." The State Court intoned that the sentiments of those thinking otherwise [*Andersdenkender*] were to be pro-tected without recourse as to whether they were objectively justified. "In things of sentiment, of conviction, there is no position from which it could be determined with general effect whether they are objectively right." "To treat other notions with care, *precisely because they exist*, this it is which Article 148, paragraph 2 of the [Weimar] *Reich* constitution makes into a duty for instruction in public schools." Thus thinking otherwise as such became an object of protection, feeling otherwise as such – precisely because it was *other* – was protected against folkish feeling [*völkisches Empfinden*], and in this dialectic of otherness the one thinking otherwise, feeling otherwise and typologically other [*Andersgeartete*] generally became the defined point of relation of public life and the central figure of the "basic rights" of an "other" Germany.

But out of a yet further, no less decisive, ground, the Weimar constitution had to remain a mere shadow. Before and after the War in Germany one grounded the demand for a democratic constitution with the claim that the general equal military duty and the general equal voting right indivisibly belong together. This proposition is oft put, which, in this abstract generality is mostly misleading because the democracies of the different peoples and times are not comparable, and in particular the typical liberal democracy of the nineteenth century is something essentially other than a political democracy in the pre-liberal sense. The word democracy labels many typologically different political systems. A general military duty can also be bound up with typologically different army constitutions (standing army in peacetime or militia). In any case, the liberal democracy of the Weimar Republic without the general military duty contained a double contradiction in itself. Against the Prussian soldier state, according to its ancestry out of the longstanding battle against this state, the Weimar Republic could only have justified itself historically and morally in that it carried forth undaunted or even augmented the soldierly and warrior qualities of the German people, its courage and its military will. In place of this, it became the instrument of disarmament and of subjection. No less was the contradiction with regard to the general ideology of the Western democracies, to whose basic principles one subjected oneself, in order to free oneself from the reproach of Prussian militarism and to become a typologically equal [*artgleiches*] member of the liberal democratic civilizational society. The Western liberal democracies had won the war, but the "other" Germany subjected itself not only to its constitutional ideal, but also simultaneously to the Dictate of Versailles, which abolished the general military duty and the German General Staff. The constitutional concept of the Western powers triumphed only at the cost of Germany; the existential mutual relation between the army and complete state constitution was disregarded, and this Weimar system believed that it could be a people's state without a people's army, a weaponless democracy. One attempted to organize a general right to vote without a general military duty, a general state citizenry without general state service – an astounding monstrosity.

The Weimar constitution was also a compromise. But the partners of this new compromise were typologically other [*anders geartet*] than those of the constitutional compromises of 1848 and 1867. There no longer stood two distinguishable opponents, Prussian soldier state and bourgeois civil constitutional state, against one another, but rather a multiplicity of typologically different parties and associations coalescing themselves into changing majorities. The complete structure of the new state essence was no longer dualistic, but it brought with it even less the promised unity. It became pluralistic. The dualism of soldier and bourgeois citizen fell away; in its place there now stood numerous fixedly organized oppositions and differences set against one another; nationalists, super- and inter-nationalists; bourgeois and

Marxists; Catholics, Evangelicals and atheists; capitalists and communists. Under the reservation of their party aims, they concluded compromises and coalitions on the questions of the German destiny. The word "pluralism" is here not an external and superficial label of some multitude of groupings, as exists with the manifold of social life everywhere and at all times, but rather a precise technical expression of state and constitutional theory. It labels a specific type of relation between state and society, a definite structure of social life in its relation to the political unity. This system developed itself in a typical way for a definite stage of bourgeois civil society, in a time, in which a multiplicity of trade unions, cartels, religious societies and other social and cultural associations and organizations, each upon its own domain, upon the formal legal basis of liberal freedoms, out of the sphere of the social and of the private, rule public life and make the political unity into a waste product of their daily compromises. Indeed, the daily compromise and the alternating questions and domains of public life for the alternating party coalitions is the method of politically constructing the will of this pluralistic system.[30]

4.

This pluralistic system grips all state institutions and transforms them into staging points and power positions of the different parties. However, it also grips the societal institutions and compels them to "politicize" themselves. It is

[30] Carl Schmitt, *Der Hüter der Verfassung* (Tübingen, 1931), p. 97; *Europäische Revue*, February 1933; Paul Ritterbusch, *Der Verfassungskompromiß von Weimar, das Experiment der Präsidialregierung und die nationalsozialistische Staatsidee* (Wittenberg, 1932).

difficult to reckon what would have become of Germany, when the pluralistic partition of the stately substance had also gripped the German army, the *Reichswehr*.[xxvii] Just as for the state civil service there were here three possibilities: either a *partition* amongst the coalition parties according to the law of the quota or of party-political parity; or an *introduction* of the army into the system, in the way that army and civil service, bound together or severed, would become fellow players in this pluralism and would enter themselves in to the daily compromise as coalition partners or compromise partners; or finally the attempt to play the role of a *neutral*, and therefore *higher third*, balancing umpire between the oppositions of the political parties and the different organizations. Were this pluralistic party system to coincide with the general military duty – whether with the pre-War organization of a standing army, whether with a militia organization – then it would have been inlaid into the logic of such a state structure, just as with the German people, to parcel out the people's army to the parties as well. Finally every coalition party would have held sway over their part of armed power, and the most terrible of civil wars would have been unavoidable.

It was an achievement of the German Reichswehr, under the leadership of the President of the *Reich* and its military brass to build a party-politically neutral power and in this way, throughout times of open or latent civil war, through the dangerous stage of such a pluralism, to uphold the German state. From the vantage of state law, this was made possible via a state legal construction of the President of the *Reich* as guardian of the constitution, emerging from a state political consciousness of responsibility and clear knowledge of the concrete constitutional situation, with a sensible interpretation both of the concept of the constitution as well as of the extraordinary competences of Article 48. As in the time of the conflict, the Prussian King, so now a Prussian General Field Marshall, out of his existential bond with the Prussian–German soldier state, found, in the security of silence, the path which opened a transition to other constitutional conditions. On 20 July 1932, the President of the *Reich*, under simultaneous promulgation of the martial state of exception [*militärischer Ausnahmezustand*], on the basis of Article 48, removed the directing Weimar coalitional government in Prussia from its office. Therewith, the Prussian state was struck from the hand of the Weimar system. So far did the force of the old state still reach, and the day of this Prussian coup d'état [*Preußenschlag*] remains a glorious day for the German Reichswehr. In a pluralistic party system it was able to enact and hold pure its claim to *neutrality* and nonpartisanship. But the *claim to totality* [*Totalitätsanspruch*],[xxviii] which pertains to all political leadership [*Führung*], it couldn't even once raise, much less enact, although the state-bearing function, which in ascending measure it was compelled to perceive, constantly necessitated it to do so, and the legality of a constitution of the type of the Weimar compromise would have to destroy every attempt at renewal of this type in its first beginnings, like a cadaverous poison.

When 20 June 1932 and the liquidation of the Weimar government in Prussia had also shown that even the weak remnant of the Prussian–German soldier state was still superior to the bourgeois civil constitutional usufructuaries of the collapse of 1918, then its political force did not yet suffice to lead the German *Reich* politically. The *Reich* had to allow itself to be drawn before the bar of the

Staatsgerichtshof in Leipzig by the Ministers of the Weimar system removed from their offices and by some typologically equal [*gleichgearteten*] state governments. There the *Reich* had to answer as "accused" for a political decision before an instance whose whole claim to authority was only based upon its wishing to be fully unpolitical. Even the stage of constitutional justiciability still pertains to the consequential course of a bourgeois civil constitutionalism, which destroys every possibility of an authentic government.

In the Second *Reich*, the restrictions advanced for political necessities based upon the budgetary right of the parliament still had a political claim to leadership [*Führungsanspruch*] as its basis, and when this parliamentary government accusably renounced, when they should have justified their claim to leadership, so there lay in the demand for a parliamentary government at least in thought still no full negation of the concept of leadership and government in general. And when the totality of the political decision was laid claim to from the side of budgetary right, thus from the economic and financial side, then this was a claim, which was based upon a factual responsibility and upon an important matter. But when only the normativism of a constitution is to be valid, and neither a dynastic, nor a democratic, nor any other type of legitimacy is present, but only a value neutral legality, all political governmental decisions are subjected to the purportedly pure juristic judgment of an instance, which for its part is responsible and subjected to Nobody other than a highly unclear statute to be interpreted by itself. Then a court, filled with independent, i.e. not responsible, irremovable, civil service judges, speaks the last word in the state. Every possibility of a government or even leadership [*Führung*] is then laid aside and the liberal democratic ideal of a *Führer-*

less rule-of-law state is realized. The professional civil service judge cannot even theoretically assert that his trial decision is government or even leadership [*Führung*]. Admittedly it is thinkable to unfurl the totality of the political decision from the juristic side as well, just as from the economic and from the financial side; because every political decision necessarily always also has a legal side, as, conversely, every legal decision always also can have a political side. But the distinction between Juristic and Political is not based upon a domain, like the economy or the military, but rather only upon the abstract, purely formal normativism of a mere legality. The methods of such a *Staatsgerichtshof* consequently at length annihilate every state authority, not only of government, but also of the *Staatsgerichtshof* itself. As it is practically and theoretically a contradiction in itself, to allow an unpolitical judge, precisely because he desires to be unpolitical, to decide upon political questions from the juristic side. The judge thereby is placed into a compulsory situation without exit: either he takes the political decision, then he raises for himself the impossible claim that the political opinion of a civil service judge is something Higher than the political opinion of a political *Führer*; or he declines the decision out of a feeling of political responsibility and thereby places himself under the objection of withholding the law.

CONCLUSION

That in the last stage of the Weimar system a trial-shaped decisive court emerged as the highest political instance of the German *Reich* and sat in judgment in the contortions of a political trial concerning justice and injustice, honor and dishonor of the *Reich*'s President and of the *Reich*'s government, therein the bourgeois civil constitutionalism of the nineteenth century fulfilled itself. In the Weimar constitution of 1919, it found its system purified of all "nonconstitutional" elements. After the renunciation of the parliamentary government it developed of itself toward political subjection under the neutrality of unpolitical judges, who not only did not claim to lead or to govern politically, but rather, on the contrary, precisely based their competence and their right of decision on the ground that they indignantly repudiated every political claim to leadership. Thus, bourgeois civil constitutionalism consequently thought out to the end found its peak point precisely there, where the zero point of the will to political leadership lay. This was the fulfillment and crowning of bourgeois civil constitutional thought.

The salvation of Germany could not come out of the system of such legality. It came out of the German people itself, out of the National Socialist movement, which emerged in resistance against the powers of the collapse of 1918. Already that *Preußenschlag* of 20 July 1932 was only thereby possible because the National Socialist movement pressed forth irresistibly. On 30 January 1933, the General Field Marshall of the German army in the World War named a German soldier, however, precisely a *political* soldier, Adolf Hitler, to the Chancellorship of the German *Reich*. That the *Führer* of an emerging movement laying claim to totality became German *Reich*'s Chancellor already lay beyond the concepts of a liberal democratic constitutional system. Thereby, that the whole state power of the German *Reich* was given into the hand of such a *Führer*, the first step was accordingly made upon a new constitutional soil [*Verfassungsboden*]. Now a path opened itself in order to take clear internal political decisions, to free the German people from the hundred years' bewilderment of bourgeois civil constitutionalism and, in place of normative constitutional facades, to embark upon the revolutionary work of a German state order.

Appendix

Carl Schmitt, "The Logic of Spiritual Subjection" [1934][*]

1.

It was the sense of the "constitutional" monarchy of the German nineteenth century to attempt a compromise and a bridging over of the oppositions between German soldier state and bourgeois civil constitutional state.

But only in the smaller and middling states of Germany, which were not, like Prussia, the bearers of a great historical mission, and which could thus more easily accommodate themselves to external decision, was a real compromise possible and was it attained. In Prussia, the leading German state, the complete state structure remained defined into its foundations by the opposition which forever divides a soldier state from a bourgeois civil constitutional state. In the year 1848, even the soldier state Prussia saw itself

---

* This article contains some thoughts of a lecture held on 24 January 1934 in the Berlin University, "Heerwesen und staatliche Gesamtstruktur" ["Army and the Complete State Structure"], as well as of a treatise soon to appear, "Staatliche Struktur und Zusammenbruch des zweiten Reiches; der Sieg des Bürgers über den Soldaten" ["Stately Structure and Collapse of the Second Empire; the Victory of the Bourgeois Citizen over the Soldier"].

pressed toward the "constitutional solution." But it thereby brought itself into a self-destructive predicament: it could not overcome the cleft, but had to cover it over via persistently victorious wars and uninterruptedly increasing economic prosperity. Only in this way was it possible to retain the illusion of an attained constitutional compromise and of a synthesis between soldier and bourgeois citizen.

The Prussian soldier state defended itself courageously. It was able to hold the military supreme command [*Kommandogewalt*] free from ministerial countersignature and thereby to take the army out of the domain of the bourgeois civil constitutional system. In the half-hundred years' strife concerning the scope of the supreme command, in particular concerning the ministerial countersignature for the appointment and dismissal of officers, and concerning military justiciability, Prussia upheld its soldierly standpoint. The army was withdrawn from the political consequences of the liberal constitutional state. Yet with this, the fatal cleft of the complete state structure was not overcome, but only further sharpened. The army was isolated, a "state within the state," and in the situation had to *renounce* raising beyond its own frame with regard to the whole German people the *total leadership claim* [*totalen Führungsanspruch*], which pertains to all political leadership and to every decision. Indeed, the general military duty stood, and the army was still "the great educational school of the nation," but the concept of education of German bourgeois civil society was other than that of the Prussian soldier state. In the open collision of these "educational" claims, the army modestly retreated. The army should and sought to be the educational school for the nation *only for war*, and war appeared to the thought of this century as a case seldom occurring, as an extreme and isolated occasion, swiftly laid to rest. The claim to be an "educational school," and the claim to training and leading following from it thus regrettably related, as an exemplary officer strikingly noted, only to the *ultima ratio*,[i] only to a case imagined to be abnormal, and not, in any sense exceeding the narrowest disciplinary frame of the military, to the complete real life of the German people. "The preparation for *battle* is the main task of military training."[1] From decade to decade one habituated oneself almost unconsciously to the view that the army was a matter for itself, precisely that "state within the state" only stepping into action for the most extreme case. It withdrew into itself and was already on this ground spiritually in an almost fraught defensive position.

In a state of such a "constitution" the soldierly part, the core of the state, stood upon a lost post. The constitution itself, the basic law, the basic agreement, the fundamental "compromise," was concluded at the exclusive cost of the soldier state. "Constitution" in the German nineteenth century meant essentially not only a restriction of the kingly competencies of power, but rather above all a negation of the basic propositions and consequences of the Prussian soldier state. This was the inner basic law according to which monarchic constitutionalism was mustered up in Prussia and under which it had to develop further with irresistible logic. The originary compromise, which such a constitution represented, had to proceed in ever further compromises of the same structure, with ever further diminutions

---

[1] Compare Moltke's written reflection of 25 July 1868 and the secret "Instruction for the higher troop-leaders" based upon it from 24 June 1869 (Moltke, *Taktisch-strategische Aufsätze*, p. 67; Curt Jany, *Geschichte der Königlich Preußischen Armee*, vol. IV., 1933, p. 257).

of the soldier state. Every statute, every annual budget, every agreement between government and parliament concerning military strength in peacetime or related matters confirmed and expanded the power of the popular representation over the constitution, and lent it, even when it yielded and conceded to the government, new arguments and legal titles. Every concession, within the logic of such a constitutional situation, to the military demands of the government endangered the parties that were willing to make them, and made them defenseless against the cheap trumps of the "Left" parties. The law of development, to which the Prussian state gave itself over, as it allowed itself this kind of "constitution," could only work itself out *against* the Prussian state. Tremendous military and foreign policy successes altered nothing in this and, at most, could effect a postponement. Victorious wars, the likes of which world-history little knows, helped this Prussian soldier state to uphold itself in internal policy, to conceal the conflict, to attain the exemption of the supreme command [*Kommandogewalt*] and a delay of the open conflict. A parliament, which had done everything to make the victory impossible, against whose loud cry and public contradiction the army organization sustained itself and achieved the victory, conferred upon the victor the retroactive permission and "indemnity."

King Wilhelm the First recognized the decisive point of the fraught situation of the Prussian state, the military supreme command [*Kommandogewalt*], and upheld it with heroic fixity. The more that both the particularities and backgrounds of the history of the battle between the Prussian soldier state and the liberal movement become known to us, the more the figure of this king grows into a world-historical grandeur. His superiority was noiseless. It was not the superiority of an ingenious individual, but rather the superiority of a man integrated into the super-individual historical context, who holds fast to a line, which was only recognizable to him by force of his self-evident unity with the Prussian state. In a century which was filled with the noise of liberal constitutional legal discussions, he heard only the voice of the duty to the state, and, namely to the Prussian soldier state. Only thereby did he find the force to retain the great and ingenious men, who brought the work to fulfillment: Bismarck, Moltke and Roon. But even the King pressed for beseeching the parliament for "indemnity" after the victorious war, and held this for legality. Even he, without becoming conscious of the bearing of his deed, in the fullness of feeling, and with the generosity of the victor, spiritually subjected himself.

2.

The World War began for us Germans with a terrible spiritual subjection and defeat. The battle against Russian "Czarism" was taken over officially as a war aim: therein expressed itself the lack of spiritual resistance against the constitutional ideology of Western liberal democracy and the internal political enemies of the Prussian soldier state. But the subjection went further. On 4 August 1914 the Chancellor of the German *Reich*, Bethmann Hollweg, declared in his speech before the Reichstag that the march of the German army into Belgium was an *unjust*[ii] act, which one had to repair. A childish jurisprudence in the service of a *policy running after the [good] impression of enemy foreign countries* caused this ignominious capitulation.

The cleft in the inner-state structure broke out during the World War and ground down the force of resistance.

Foreign descriptions of the rapport between war-leading and state-leading for the World War 1914–18 gladly proceed upon the assumption that the relation between military power and civil power, army brass and government, was in no way a serious organizational problem for Germany during the war, because the Kaiser as supreme commander had an unrestricted power in a nonparliamentarily governed state.[2] This is a superficial view, which is based upon an errant exaggeration of the distinction between constitutional and parliamentary monarchy. In truth the exemption of the supreme command [*Kommandogewalt*] of the Kaiser from the bourgeois civil constitutional system even during the war remained a sign that the complete structure of the state was clefted and this cleft deepened itself with the augmenting expansion and intensity of the World War. The totality of the war aim enacted itself in every war-waging land. This totality cannot be isolated, but rather is laid claim to out of every domain. Consequently, it expresses itself not only as a total claim of war-waging, but rather also as a total claim of political state leadership, and of economic leadership. During the World War the German constitutional situation was of the kind that the emerging differences in all war-waging states between army brass and government, military and civil responsibility, had to work themselves out in Germany in a state- and people-destroying way in internal politics.

The inner cleft of the complete structure of the Second *Reich*, which the opposition between Prussian soldier state and bourgeois constitutional state only concealed and delayed,

---

[2] Thus, for example: J.M. Bourget, *Gouvernement et Commandement* [Les Leçons de la Guerre Mondiale] (Paris: Payot, 1930).

which was not overcome, emerged openly in the World War, as the military situation became difficult. Every political difference between the *Reich*'s Chancellor and a leader of the army touched immediately upon the last roots of this internal political dualism. The wars of 1864, 1866, and 1870 took a swift and victorious course, but still they allowed the thoroughly isolated internal political defensive situation of the core of the soldier state to be known. During the World War every worsening of the military or foreign policy situation redounded in inner-state matters with almost mathematic exactitude to the benefit of the counterpart, the parliament, and lent it constitutional legal arguments for new claims to power. With the growing danger, instead of the internal political unity of the German people growing stronger and more fixed, the logic of the constitutional structure and of the constitutional dualism of soldier and bourgeois citizen, then, too, of soldier and (following the bourgeois citizen) worker worked in the opposite direction. Every disappointment, every difficulty of waging war gave the arguments of the opposition of 1866, only appeased via a splendid foreign policy success, retrospective right and ripped open anew the conflict which had only been covered over via a victorious war. The unresolved contradiction of the inner-state complete structure, the opposition of the Prussian soldier state against a bourgeois civil constitutional state, the hard fact, that the actual constitutional compromise was only based upon the *victorious* war, all this deepened in the compulsion of such a constitutional system with the growing difficulties of the situation of the World War into the opposition between government and people and finally into the fatal opposition between army and homeland, soldier and worker. On this, Germany collapsed.

The liberal bourgeois citizenry could indeed come to terms with the army and with war after the successes of 1866 and 1870, but precisely only so long as they were victorious and successful. To this authentically bourgeois civil claim to successful wars and economic prosperity, the Prussian soldier state spiritually subjected itself, as it in 1866 after the victorious wars bade the parliament for "indemnity" and received it. Therewith was the legal claim of the liberal movement recognized and the law of the further historical development of Prussia and Germany defined. War is in no way generally and unconditionally negated by a liberal bourgeoisie; a "victorious war" can even be held by it as "socially ideal," but naturally only a *victorious* war. No state, in any case, and least of all a state of the structure of Prussia, can seriously go in for such claims and "ideals"; no institution, and least of all the political unity of a people, may establish itself only upon the convenient case and make its type of existence dependent upon uninterrupted lucky successes. Should the luck once run out, should the war once cease to be successful, then the basic presupposition of the "constitutional compromise" would fall away; the bourgeois citizen would have to feel himself deceived and would demand as his good right the consequent liberal democratic constitutional state, wherewith it is wholly equipollent whether the singular liberals as individuals were well-meaning patriotic people or not. They were certainly all good and honest bourgeois citizens. But they all stood under the law of their political movement and under the compulsion which they themselves induced of the internal political complete structure of the Prussian state.

3.

In the year 1806 there collapsed the organization of an army thwarted upon the open field of battle and only as a consequence of this collapse did the stately organization pertaining to this army collapse. In 1918 the army fighting on the front was undefeated, but a cleft of the internal state structure concealed and thereby unrecognized in its real significance for fifty years broke out, in the critical moment, destructively. Not federal and confederal state tensions, but rather this inner-state and inner-Prussian constitutional problematic displayed itself as the ominous onset for the internal breach of the political unity of a people battling against the world.

In 1918, Western liberal democracy had won. The Weimar constitution of 1919 gave the inner-German answer of the bourgeois citizenry to the *non*-victorious war; the retroactive answer only concealed and delayed in 1866 for the *other* case. With this constitution Germany subjected itself to the democratic constitutional ideal of its enemies and simultaneously to the Dictate of Versailles, which laid aside the general military duty and the German General Staff. One took over the legal and constitutional ideal of the triumphing Western powers. Helpless and defenseless one even disregarded the existential mutual relation between the essence of the army and the complete state constitution. One hoped that one could be a weaponless democracy. One sought to organize a general right to vote without a general military duty, a general state citizenship without general state duty – an astounding monstrosity. But the good impression in foreign countries was achieved, and the specialists of this good impression felt themselves as the internal political victors and gave a posthumous answer to the constitutional problems of the Prussian conflict of 1862–1866.

The courageous and in the war victorious Prussian soldier state stood throughout a whole century in a fraught defensive, indeed, in full defenselessness. Its political opponents dominated the language and the concepts of the time. To them alone redounded the argument of the "impression in foreign countries." Victorious wars, state achievements of unexampled grandeur were thereby brought to their historical benefit. In *three decisive moments* of the history of the last century the spiritual subjection under the legal conception of the opponent inauspiciously defined the fate of Germany. First apparently unimportant and apparently not decisive in the year 1866, as one believed one could afford it, with the superiority of the victor and in the moment of success to beseech the liberal opposition for indemnity and to subject itself to their concepts of law and constitution. The second moment was already more dangerous and nearer to the catastrophe: the Chancellor of the German *Reich* saw the spiritual justification of the World War in the battle against Czarism; he declared the German march into Belgium as "unjust" and betrayed the army of the German people to the constitutional ideals and legal concepts of its external and internal political enemies. The third moment finally fulfilled this development: in the collapse of 1918 the ideas of the liberal democratic constitutional state first triumphed in internal politics over the spirit of the German people and then also militarily and in foreign policy as well and effected the disarmament of the battling army.

These three moments stand in a single composite line of development. In their succession a law consequently unfolds itself: first the internal political spiritual subjection of the

Prussian soldier state under the legal concepts of the bourgeois civil rule-of-law and constitutional state; then the subjection under the spiritual war aim of the enemy, bound up with the subaltern striving to a make a good impression in foreign countries and to appease the enemy via spiritual yielding and "objectivity"; and finally the open highly treasonous and land-betraying subjection under the state- and legal ideals of a precisely thereby victorious, merciless enemy. The logic of spiritual subjection fulfilled itself in a defenseless and resistanceless political servitude.

Notes

Foreword by Reinhard Mehring

i These are collectedly available in Carl Schmitt, *Gesammelte Schriften 1933–1936 mit ergänzenden Beiträgen aus der Zeit des Zweiten Weltkriegs* (Berlin: Duncker & Humblot, 2021).

ii On this, the letters of Bilfinger of 24 September 1933; 14 February and 31 May 1934 to Schmitt, in *Der Staats- und Völkerrechtler Carl Bilfinger (1879–1958). Dokumentation seiner politischen Biographie*, ed. Philipp Glahé et al. (Baden-Baden: Nomos Verlag, 2024), p. 179ff.

iii Carl Schmitt, *Tagebücher 1930–1934*, ed. Wolfgang Schuller and Gerd Giesler (Berlin: Akademie Verlag, 2010), p. 342.

iv Question from Gretha Jünger to Schmitt on 31 March 1934 in Gretha Jünger-Carl Schmitt, *Briefwechsel 1934–1953*, ed. Ingeborg Villinger and Alexander Jaser (Berlin: Akademie Verlag, 2007), p. 24.

v Schmitt on 15 March 1934 to Gretha Jünger, in Gretha Jünger–Carl Schmitt, *Briefwechsel*, p. 23.

vi Schmitt, *Staatsgefüge und Zusammenbruch des zweiten Reiches*, ed. Günter Maschke (Berlin: Duncker & Humblot, 2011), p. 29.

vii Ernst Jünger, *Der Arbeiter. Herrschaft und Gestalt* (Hamburg: Hanseatische Verlagsanstalt, 1932); cf. Jünger, *Typus, Name, Gestalt* (Stuttgart: Klett, 1963).

viii Carl Schmitt–Ernst Rudolf Huber, *Briefwechsel 1926–1981 Mit ergänzenden Materialien*, ed. Ewald Grothe (Berlin: Duncker & Humblot, 2014), p. 173.

  ix Carl Schmitt, *Verfassungslehre* (Berlin: Duncker & Humblot, 2017 [1928]), p. 4.

   x Carl Schmitt, *Der Begriff des Politischen* (Berlin: Duncker & Humblot, 1963), p. 46.

  xi Oswald Spengler, *Preußentum und Sozialismus* (1919), in Spengler, *Politische Schriften* (Munich: Beck, 1933), pp. 1–105.

  xii On this, compare Schmitt, "Der Staat des 20. Jahrhunderts," in *Gesammelte Schriften 1933–1936*, pp. 36–38, at p. 37.

 xiii Walter Benjamin, *Das Kunstwerk im Zeitalter seiner technischen Reproduzierbarkeit*, in Benjamin, *Schriften*, vol. I/2, pp. 469, 508.

 xiv On this, see above all Schmitt's diary entries from 17 to 18 May 1948 in *Glossarium* (Berlin: Duncker & Humblot, 2015), p. 114f.

  xv Schmitt, *Staatsgefüge*, p. 35.

 xvi Schmitt, *Staatsgefüge*, p. 30.

 xvii Schmitt, *Tagebücher 1930–1934*, p. 252.

xviii See above all the critique by Fritz Hartung in *Historische Zeitschrift* 151 (1935), pp. 528–544; on this see also the exemplary study of Hans-Christof Krauss, "Soldatenstaat oder Verfassungsstaat? – Zur Kontroverse zwischen Carl Schmitt und Fritz Hartung über den preußisch-deutschen Konstitutionalismus (1934/35)," in *Jahrbuch für die Geschichte Mittel- und Ostdeutschlands* 45 (1999), pp. 275–310; more generally, Ewald Grothe, *Zwischen Geschichte und Recht. Deutsche Verfassungsgeschichtsschreibung 1900–1970* (Munich: Oldenbourg, 2005).

 xix Schmitt, *Staatsgefüge*, p. 39.

  xx On this, Carl Schmitt, "Was bedeutet der Streit um den ‚Rechtsstaat'," in *Gesammelte Schriften 1933–1936*, pp. 296–307, at p. 296; compare also Schmitt, "Der Führer schützt das Recht," in *Gesammelte Schriften 1933–1936*, pp. 200–204, p. 201 ("kraft seines Führertums als oberster Gerichtsherr unmittelbar Recht schafft"), p. 203 ("unmittelbares Führerhandeln").

xxi On this, see the expanded edition by Helmuth Kiesel (ed.), Ernst Jünger, *Auf den Marmorklippen* (Stuttgart: Klett-Cotta, 2017).

xxii Der Nachlass Carl Schmitts im Landesarchiv NRW Abt. Rheinland (Bestand RW 0265), item number 29071 (hereafter in the form RW 265-29071).

xxiii Max Weber, Rezension von Erich Kaufmann, *Bismarcks Erbe in der Reichsverfassung* (Berlin: Julius Springer, 1917) in the *Frankfurter Zeitung* of 28 October 1917, reprinted in Weber, *Gesammelte Politische Schriften* (Tübingen: J.C.B. Mohr, 1980 [Fourth Edition]), pp. 241–244.

xxiv Carl Schmitt, *Theorie des Partisanen* (Berlin: Duncker & Humblot, 1963), p. 95.

xxv Carl Schmitt, *Ex Captivitate Salus* (Cologne: Greven Verlag, 1950), p. 38ff.

xxvi Carl Schmitt, *Das Zeitalter der Neutralisierungen und Entpolitisierungen* in Carl Schmitt, *Der Begriff des Politischen* (Berlin: Duncker & Humblot, 1963), p. 93.

xxvii Reinhard Mehring, ed., *"Auf der gefahrenvollen Straße des öffentlichen Rechts"; Briefwechsel Carl Schmitt – Rudolf Smend, 1921–1961. Mit ergänzenden Materialien* (Berlin: Duncker & Humblot, 2012 [2010]), p. 178.

xxviii On this, Herfried Münkler, *Der Wandel des Krieges. Von der Symmetrie zur Asymmetrie* (Weilerswist: Velbrück Wissenschaft, 2006); most recently, Herfried Münkler, *Macht im Umbruch. Deutschlands Rolle in Europa und die Herausforderungen des 21. Jahrhunderts* (Berlin: Rowohlt, 2025).

xxix Ernst Rudolf Huber, *Heer und Staat in der deutschen Geschichte* (Hamburg: Hanseatische Verlagsanstalt, 1938).

State Composition and Collapse of the Second Reich

i "Adolf Hitler" is italicized here in Schmitt's German original. [Ed.]

ii Schmitt's German here is "politische Gestaltung," which might less literally be rendered as "political form" (although Schmitt is not using the exact same vocabulary as in his 1923 pamphlet with that phrase in the title). [Ed.]

iii King Frederick II of Prussia (1712–1786) published a selection of his writings in French under the title *Oeuvres du Philosophe de Sans Souci* in 1749–1750, with Sans Souci (alt. Sanssouci) being Frederick's summer palace in Potsdam, built in the years preceding the publication of these writings. [Ed.]

iv *Kriegführung*, alternately, leadership in war. [Ed.]

v On the Saverne or Zabern Affair of 1913, which concerned German warrantless arrests and the military administration in Alsace–Lorraine, see Christopher Clark, *Kaiser Wilhelm II: A Life in Power* (London: Penguin, 2009 [2000]), pp. 160–161: "Far more damaging to the reputation of the German administration in Alsace-Lorraine and to the political standing of the Bethmann administration was the celebrated 'Zabern Affair' that broke out in October 1913, when insulting remarks by a German officer set off a train of minor clashes with the local population that culminated in the illegal arrest of some twenty citizens on 28 November. Here again, the conflict turned on divergent understandings of how the administration should handle its relations with the local inhabitants. The military leadership in the province took the view that insubordinate behaviour posed a direct threat to the prestige and effectiveness of the military and supported the action taken by the officer who had ordered the arrests. The civil administration, by contrast, blamed the military for exacerbating the political climate in the region by its provocative and insensitive behaviour. Once again, Wilhelm sided with the military; while he expressly pledged his support to Corps Commander von Deimling, he sent Wedel a telegram in which he laid responsibility for the deterioration in the province at the door of the civil administration." [Ed.]

vi Latin in Schmitt's German original: "Father, I have sinned." [Ed.]

vii This phrase ("*Lücke in der Verfassung*") is italicized in Schmitt's German original. [Ed.]

viii This quote is italicized in Schmitt's German original. [Ed.]

ix See Genesis 25:34, which runs (in the King James Version): "Then Jacob gave Esau bread and pottage of lentils; and he did eat and drink, and rose up, and went his way: thus, Esau despised his birthright." For the pottage of lentils, Esau sells his birthright as first-born son of Isaac. The Luther Bible gives "Linsengericht" for "pottage of lentils" in this same passage, to which Schmitt's "*Linsengericht* einer fremden Legalität" refers. [Ed.]

x Linsengericht – pottage of lentils: see Genesis 25:28–34. "[28] Und Isaak hatte Esau lieb und aß gern von seinem Weidwerk; Rebekka aber hatte Jakob lieb.[29] Und Jakob kochte ein Gericht. Da kam Esau vom Felde und war müde[30] und sprach zu Jakob: Laß mich kosten das rote Gericht; denn ich bin müde. Daher heißt er Edom.[31] Aber Jakob sprach: Verkaufe mir heute deine Erstgeburt.[32] Esau antwortete: Siehe, ich muß doch sterben; was soll mir denn die Erstgeburt?[33] Jakob sprach: So schwöre mir heute. Und er schwur ihm und verkaufte also Jakob seine Erstgeburt.[34] Da gab ihm Jakob Brot und das Linsengericht, und er aß und trank und stand auf und ging davon. Also verachtete Esau seine Erstgeburt." [Ed.]

xi "Other and Deeper" ("Anderes und Tieferes") is abnormally capitalized in all editions of Schmitt's German original, which emphasis is retained in the translation above. [Ed.]

xii Even under the German Kaiser, there were still separate armies which swore allegiance to their respective princes. [Ed.]

xiii "Supreme commander," here, renders *Oberster Kriegsherr* (literally, Highest Warlord), an attribute of the Kaiser's official power. [Ed.]

xiv Schmitt here appears to refer to a terminological reference work of administrative law, Karl von Stengel (ed.),

Wörterbuch des Deutschen Verwaltungsrechts. In Verbindung mit vielen Gelehrten und höheren Beamten, Vol. I. Freiburg, i. B., J. C. B. Mohr (Paul Siebeck, 1890). [Ed.]

 xv The first two volumes of Bismarck's memoirs, *Gedanken und Erinnerungen* [*Thoughts and Reminiscences*], were published posthumously in late 1898 after Bismarck's death in July of that year. [Ed.]

 xvi "Re intellecta, in verbis simus faciles" – once something is known, it is easy to put into words. Latin in Schmitt's (and Bismarck's) German original. [Ed.]

 xvii Latin in Schmitt's German original, final reason, ultimate reason, or, in context, a final instance. [Ed.]

 xviii "Other" [*ein Anderer*] is irregularly capitalized in Schmitt's German original in all editions. [Ed.]

 xix "Nearer [one]" [*des Näheren*] is irregularly capitalized (and thereby substantivized) in Schmitt's German original in all editions. [Ed.]

 xx Latin in Schmitt's German original: indirect power. [Ed.]

 xxi French in Schmitt's German original: the king reigns and does not govern. [Ed.]

 xxii Schmitt's German here is "konstitutionellen Verfassung," rendered as constitutional order above; the literal rendering would be "constitutional constitution." [Ed.]

 xxiii See Maschke's notes in Schmitt, *Staatsgefüge* (2011 [1934]), p. 86 note 65. [Ed.]

 xxiv More literally, this sentence might read: "It expresses itself consequentially not only as totality claim of war leading [*Kriegführung*], but rather also as totality claim of political state-leading [*Staatsführung*] and equally of leading the economy [*Wirtschaftsführung*]." [Ed.]

 xxv The cross-reference is relativized to the pagination changes between the 1934 and 2011 editions of the German text. [Ed.]

 xxvi French and italicized in Schmitt's German original: the absence of the king. [Ed.]

 xxvii *Reichswehr* is italicized here in Schmitt's German original. [Ed.]

xxviii Both *neutrality* [*Neutralität*] and *claim to totality* [*Totalitätsanspruch*] are italicized in Schmitt's German original. [Ed.]

Appendix

This article by Carl Schmitt originally appeared in the 1 March 1934 issue of *Deutsches Volkstum* 16:5, pp. 177–182. The article is reprinted as an appendix in Günter Maschke's edition of Schmitt's *Staatsgefüge und Zusammenbruch des zweiten Reiches* (Berlin: Duncker & Humblot, 2011), pp. 109–117 and in Carl Schmitt, *Gesammelte Schriften 1933–1936* (Berlin: Duncker & Humblot, 2021), pp. 148–153.

    i Latin in Schmitt's German original: ultimate aim, ultimate reason. [Ed.]

   ii Italics present in Schmitt's German original on *Unrecht* [*unjust*]. [Ed.]

Bibliography

Archival and Manuscript Sources

Der Nachlass Carl Schmitts im Landesarchiv NRW Abt. Rheinland (Bestand RW 0265), item number 29071 (RW 0265–29071) – Carl Schmitt's personal copy of *Staatsgefüge und Zusammenbruch des zweiten Reiches* (Hamburg: Hanseatische Verlagsanstalt, 1934).

Der Nachlass Carl Schmitts im Landesarchiv NRW Abt. Rheinland (Bestand RW 0265), item number 21752 (RW 0265–21752), Carl Schmitt, "Heerwesen und staatliche Gesamtstruktur," lecture manuscript.

German Editions of State Composition and Collapse of the Second Reich

Carl Schmitt, *Staatsgefüge und Zusammenbruch des zweiten Reiches* (Hamburg: Hanseatische Verlagsanstalt, 1934).

(Heft 6 of *Der deutsche Staat der Gegenwart*, Carl Schmitt ed.)

Carl Schmitt, *Staatsgefüge und Zusammenbruch des zweiten Reiches: Der Sieg des Bürgers über den Soldaten*, ed. Günter Maschke (Berlin: Duncker & Humblot, 2011 [1934]).

German-Language Sources

Konrad Barthel, *Friederich der Grosse in Hitlers Geschichtsbild* (Wiesbaden: Franz Steiner Verlag, 1977).

Carl Bilfinger, *Der Staats- und Völkerrechtler Carl Bilfinger (1879–1958). Dokumentation seiner politischen Biografie*, ed. Philipp Glahé et al. (Baden-Baden: Nomos Verlag, 2024).

Dirk Blasius, *Carl Schmitt: Preußischer Staatsrat in Hitlers Reich* (Göttingen: Vandenhoeck & Ruprecht, 2001).

Dirk Blasius, "Carl Schmitt und der 'Heereskonflikt' des Dritten Reiches," *Historische Zeitschrift*, 281 (2005), pp. 659–682.

Dirk Blasius, *Carl Schmitt und der 30. Januar 1933* (Frankfurt: Peter Lang, 2009).

Arthur Moeller van den Bruck, *Das dritte Reich* (Hamburg: Hanseatische Verlagsanstalt, 1931).

Kai Burkhardt (ed.), *Carl Schmitt und die Öffentlichkeit; Briefwechsel mit Journalisten, Publizisten und Verlegern aus den Jahren 1923 bis 1983* (Berlin: Duncker & Humblot, 2013).

Gerd Giesler, "Nachwort," in Carl Schmitt, *Gespräch über die Macht und den Zugang zum Machthaber*, ed. Gerd Giesler (Stuttgart: Klett-Cotta, 2008), pp. 67–95.

Ruth Groh, *Carl Schmitts gnostischer Dualismus; Der boshafte Schöpfer dieser Welt hat es so eingerichtet (. . .)* (Berlin-Münster: LIT Verlag, 2014).

Raphael Gross, *Carl Schmitt und die Juden; Eine deutsche Rechtslehre* (Durchgesehene und erweiterte Ausgabe) (Frankfurt am Main: Suhrkamp Verlag, 2005 [2000]).

Ewald Grothe, *Zwischen Geschichte und Recht. Deutsche Verfassungsgeschichtsschreibung 1900–1970* (Munich: Oldenbourg, 2005).

Ewald Grothe, "Carl Schmitt und die 'neuen Aufgaben der Verfassungsgeschichte' im Nationalsozialismus," *Forum Historiae Iuris* (2006), pp. 1–30.

Fritz Hartung, "Staatsgefüge und Zusammenbruch des zweiten Reiches," *Historische Zeitschrift* 151, no. 3 (1935), pp. 528–544.

Heinrich Heine, "Disputation," in *Romanzero, Drittes Buch: Hebräische Melodien* [1851], pp. 646–662 in Heinrich Heine,

Sämtliche Gedichte, Kommentierte Ausgabe, ed. Bernd Kortländer (Stuttgart: Philipp Reclam jun., 2009 [1990]).

Heinrich Henkel, *Strafrichter und Gesetz im neuen Staat. Die geistigen Grundlagen* (Hamburg: Hanseatische Verlagsanstalt, 1934).

Frank Hertweck and Dimitrios Kisoudis (eds.), *"Solange das Imperium da ist"; Carl Schmitt im Gespräch mit Klaus Figge und Dieter Groh 1971* (Berlin: Duncker & Humblot, 2010).

Adolf Hitler, *Mein Kampf. Eine kritische Edition*, ed. Christian Hartmann et al. (München: Institut für Zeitgeschichte, 2016).

Ernst Rudolf Huber, *Heer und Staat in der deutschen Geschichte* (Hamburg: Hanseatische Verlagsanstalt, 1938).

Ernst Jünger, *Der Arbeiter. Herrschaft und Gestalt* (Hamburg, 1932).

Ernst Jünger, *Typus, Name, Gestalt* (Stuttgart: Klett, 1963).

Ernst Jünger, *Auf den Marmorklippen* (Stuttgart: Klett-Cotta, 2017).

Ernst Kapp, *Philosophische oder Vergleichende allgemeine Erdkunde als wissenschaftliche Darstellung der Erdverhältnisse und des Menschenlebens nach ihrem inneren Zusammenhang* (2 vols.) (Braunschweig: Verlag von Georg Westermann, 1845).

Helmuth Kiesel (ed.), Ernst Jünger, *Auf den Marmorklippen* (Stuttgart: Klett-Cotta, 2017).

Victor Klemperer, *The Language of the Third Reich* (tr. Martin Brady) (London: The Athlone Press, 2000).

Otto Koellreutter, *Grundriß der Allgemeinen Staatslehre* (Tübingen: J.C.B. Mohr, 1933).

Andreas Koenen, *Der Fall Carl Schmitt* (Darmstadt: Wissenschaftliche Buchgesellschaft, 1995).

Hans-Christof Krauss, *"Soldatenstaat oder Verfassungsstaat. Zur Kontroverse zwischen Carl Schmitt und Fritz Hartung über den preußisch-deutschen Konstitutionalismus," Jahrbuch für die Geschichte Mittel- und Ostdeutschlands* 45 (1999), pp. 275–310.

Frank-Lothar Kroll, *Utopie als Ideologie. Geschichtsdenken und politisches Handeln im Dritten Reich* (Paderborn: Ferdinand Schöningh, 1998).

Dirk van Laak, "Von Alfred T. Mahan zu Carl Schmitt: Das

Verhältnis von Land- und Seemacht," Band 1.1, in *Geopolitik, Grenzgänge im Zeitgeist*, ed. I. Diekmann, P. Krüger, and J.H. Schoeps (Bände 1.1–1.2) (Potsdam: Verlag für Berlin-Brandenburg, 2000), pp. 257–282.

Dirk van Laak, *Gespräche in der Sicherheit des Schweigens; Carl Schmitt in der politischen Geistesgeschichte der frühen Bundesrepublik* (2., unveränderte Auflage) (Berlin: Akademie Verlag, 2002 [1993]).

Reinhard Mehring, "Carl Schmitt und der Antisemitismus. Ein unbekannter Text," *Forum Historiae Iuris* (2006), pp. 1–4.

Reinhard Mehring, *Carl Schmitt; Aufstieg und Fall* (München: C.H. Beck, 2009).

Reinhard Mehring, *Carl Schmitt zur Einführung* (Vierte, vollständig überarbeitete Auflage [Neufassung]) (Hamburg: Junius Verlag, 2011).

Heinrich Meier, *Die Lehre Carl Schmitts; Vier Kapitel zur Unterscheidung Politischer Theologie und Politischer Philosophie* (Dritte Auflage) (Stuttgart/Weimar: Verlag J.B. Metzler, 2009 [1994]).

Heinrich Meier, *Carl Schmitt, Leo Strauss und "Der Begriff des Politischen"; Zu einem Dialog unter Abwesenden* (Dritte Auflage) (Stuttgart/Weimar: Verlag J.B. Metzler, 2013 [1988]).

Hans Mommsen, "Preußentum und Nationalsozialismus," in *Der Nationalsozialismus. Studien zur Ideologie und Herrschaft*, ed. Wolfgang Benz, Hans Buchheim, and Hans Mommsen (Frankfurt: Fischer Taschenbuch Verlag, 1994), pp. 29–42.

Herfried Münkler, *Der Wandel des Krieges. Von der Symmetrie zur Asymmetrie* (Weilerwist: Velbrück, 2006).

Herfried Münkler, *Macht im Umbruch. Deutschlands Rolle in Europa und die Herausforderung des 21. Jahrhunderts* (Berlin: Rowohlt, 2025).

Bernd Rüthers, *Carl Schmitt im Dritten Reich, Wissenschaft als Zeitgeist-Verstärkung?* (2., erweiterte Auflage) (Munich: C.H. Beck, 1990 [1989]).

Joachim Schickel, *Gespräche mit Carl Schmitt* (Berlin: Merve Verlag, 1993).

Carl Schmitt, *Der Hüter der Verfassung* (Tübingen: Mohr, 1931).

Carl Schmitt, *Staat, Bewegung, Volk: Die Dreigliederung der politischen Einheit* (Hamburg: Hanseatische Verlagsanstalt, 1933).

Carl Schmitt, *Das Judentum in der Rechtswissenschaft, Die Deutsche Rechtswissenschaft im Kampf gegen den jüdischen Geist* (Berlin: Deutscher Rechtsverlag, 1936).

Carl Schmitt, *Land und Meer; Eine weltgeschichtliche Betrachtung* (Leipzig: Reclam, 1942).

Carl Schmitt, *Ex Captivitate Salus* (Cologne: Greven Verlag, 1950).

Carl Schmitt, *Der Begriff des Politischen* (Berlin: Duncker & Humblot, 1963).

Carl Schmitt, *Theorie des Partisanen* (Berlin: Duncker & Humblot, 1963).

Carl Schmitt, *Gesetz und Urteil; Eine Untersuchung zum Problem der Rechtspraxis* (2., unveränderte Auflage) (Munich: Verlag C.H. Beck, 1969 [1912]).

Carl Schmitt, *Land und Meer, Eine weltgeschichtliche Betrachtung* (Cologne: Hohenheim Verlag/Edition Maschke, 1981) [Dritte Auflage].

Carl Schmitt, *Glossarium. Aufzeichnungen aus den Jahren 1947–1958*, ed. Gerd Giesler and Martin Tielke (Berlin: Duncker & Humblot, 1991).

Carl Schmitt, *Das internationalrechtliche Verbrechen des Angriffskrieges und der Grundsatz "Nullum crimen, nulla poena sine lege,"* ed. Helmut Quaritsch (Berlin: Duncker & Humblot, 1994).

Carl Schmitt, *Positionen und Begriffe im Kampf mit Weimar-Genf-Versailles: 1923–1939* (Berlin: Duncker & Humblot, 1994).

Carl Schmitt, "Der bürgerliche Rechtsstaat," in *Staat, Großraum, Nomos*, ed. Günter Maschke (Berlin: Duncker & Humblot, 1995), pp. 44–54.

[Carl Schmitt], Johannes Negelinus, *Schattenrisse* [1913], in Ingeborg Villinger, *Carl Schmitts Kulturkritik der Moderne; Text, Kommentar und Analyse der "Schattenrisse" des Johannes Negelinus* (Berlin: Akademie Verlag, 1995), pp. 11–67.

Carl Schmitt, "Prolog zu 'Diálogos' (Madrid 1962)" (tr. Günter Maschke), in *Schmittiana, Beiträge zu Leben und Werk Carl*

Schmitts, Band V, ed. Piet Tommissen (Berlin: Duncker & Humblot, 1996), pp. 21–22.

Carl Schmitt, *Antworten in Nürnberg*, ed. Helmut Quaritsch (Berlin: Duncker & Humblot, 2000).

Carl Schmitt, *Der Wert des Staates und die Bedeutung des Einzelnen* (Zweite Auflage) (Berlin: Duncker & Humblot, 2004 [1914]).

Carl Schmitt, *Über die drei Arten des rechtswissenschaftlichen Denkens* (Dritte Auflage) (Berlin: Duncker & Humblot, 2006 [1934]).

Carl Schmitt, *Die Wendung zum diskriminierenden Kriegsbegriff* (Vierte Auflage) (Berlin: Duncker & Humblot, 2007 [1938]).

Carl Schmitt, *Römischer Katholizismus und politische Form* (Fünfte Auflage) (Stuttgart: Klett-Cotta, 2008 [1923]).

Carl Schmitt, *Hamlet oder Hekuba; Der Einbruch der Zeit in das Spiel* (Fünfte Auflage) (Stuttgart: Klett-Cotta, 2008 [1956]).

Carl Schmitt, *Politische Theologie II; Die Legende der Erledigung jeder Politischen Theologie* (Fünfte Auflage) (Berlin: Duncker & Humblot, 2008 [1970]).

Carl Schmitt, *Theodor Däublers "Nordlicht"; Drei Studien über die Elemente, den Geist und die Aktualität des Werkes* (Dritte Auflage) (Berlin: Duncker & Humblot, 2009 [1916]).

Carl Schmitt, *Politische Theologie* (Neunte Auflage) (Berlin: Duncker & Humblot, 2009 [1922/1934]).

Carl Schmitt, *Der Begriff des Politischen; Text von 1932 mit einem Vorwort und drei Corollarien* (8. Auflage) (Berlin: Duncker & Humblot, 2009 [1932]).

Carl Schmitt, *Völkerrechtliche Großraumordnung mit Interventionsverbot für raumfremde Mächte, Ein Beitrag zum Reichsbegriff im Völkerrecht* (Dritte, unveränderte Auflage der Ausgabe von 1941) (Berlin: Duncker & Humblot, 2009 [1941]).

Carl Schmitt, *Donoso Cortés in gesamteuropäischer Interpretation; Vier Aufsätze* (Zweite Auflage) (Berlin: Duncker & Humblot, 2009 [1950])

Carl Schmitt, *Die geistesgeschichtliche Lage des heutigen Parlamentarismus* (Berlin: Duncker & Humblot, 2010 [1923]).

Carl Schmitt, *Verfassungslehre* (Zehnte Auflage) (Berlin: Duncker & Humblot, 2010 [1928]).

Carl Schmitt, *Ex Captivitate Salus; Erfahrungen der Zeit 1945/47* (Dritte Auflage) (Berlin: Duncker & Humblot, 2010 [1950]).

Carl Schmitt, *Der Nomos der Erde im Völkerrecht des Jus Publicum Europaeum* (Fünfte Auflage) (Berlin: Duncker & Humblot, 2011 [1950]).

Carl Schmitt, *Die Tyrannei der Werte* (Dritte, korrigierte Auflage) (Berlin: Duncker & Humblot, 2011 [1967/1960]).

Carl Schmitt, *Land und Meer, Eine weltgeschichtliche Betrachtung* (Stuttgart: Klett-Cotta, 2011) [Siebte Auflage].

Carl Schmitt, *Der Leviathan in der Staatslehre des Thomas Hobbes; Sinn und Fehlschlag eines politischen Symbols* (Vierte Auflage) (Stuttgart: Klett-Cotta, 2012 [1938]).

Carl Schmitt, *Positionen und Begriffe im Kampf mit Weimar-Genf-Versailles 1923–1939* (Vierte, korrigierte Auflage) (Berlin: Duncker & Humblot, 2014 [1940]).

Carl Schmitt, *Glossarium* (Berlin: Duncker & Humblot, 2015).

Carl Schmitt, *Verfassungslehre* (Berlin: Duncker & Humblot, 2017 [1928]).

Carl Schmitt, *Gesammelte Schriften 1933–1936 mit ergänzenden Beiträgen aus der Zeit des Zweiten Weltkriegs* (Berlin: Duncker & Humblot, 2021).

Carl Schmitt, "Die Verfassung der Freiheit," *Deutsche Juristen-Zeitung* 40, no. 19 (1 October), Sp. 1133–1135, reprinted in Carl Schmitt, *Gesammelte Schriften 1933–1936* (Berlin: Duncker & Humblot, 2021), pp. 282–284.

Carl Schmitt and Álvaro d'Ors, *Briefwechsel*, ed. Montserrat Herrero (Berlin: Duncker & Humblot, 2004).

Carl Schmitt and Ernst Rudolf Huber, *Briefwechsel 1926–1981 Mit ergänzenden Materialian*, ed. Ewald Grothe (Berlin: Duncker & Humblot, 2014).

Carl Schmitt and Gretha Jünger, *Briefwechsel (1934–1953),* ed. Ingeborg Villinger and Alexander Jaser (Berlin: Akademie Verlag, 2007).

Carl Schmitt and Ernst Jünger, *Briefe 1930–1983*, ed. Helmuth

Kiesel (Zweite, ergänzte und überarbeitete Neuausgabe) (Stuttgart: Klett-Cotta, 2012 [1999]).

Carl Schmitt and Rudolf Smend, *"Auf der gefahrenvollen Straße des öffentlichen Rechts"; Briefwechsel Carl Schmitt – Rudolf Smend, 1921–1961*, ed. Reinhard Mehring (Zweite, überarbeitete Auflage) (Berlin: Duncker & Humblot, 2012 [2010]).

Carl Schmitt and Jacob Taubes, *Briefwechsel mit Materialien*, ed. Herbert Kopp-Oberstebrink, Thorsten Palzhoff, and Martin Treml (München: Wilhelm Fink, 2012).

Nicolaus Sombart, *Jugend in Berlin, 1933–1943; Ein Bericht* (Munich/Vienna: Carl Hanser Verlag, 1984).

Nicolaus Sombart, *Die deutschen Männer und ihre Feinde; Carl Schmitt – Ein deutsches Schicksal zwischen Männerbund und Matriachatsmythos* (Munich/Vienna: Carl Hanser Verlag, 1991).

Oswald Spengler, *Preußentum und Sozialismus* (Munich: C.H. Beck'sche Verlagsbuchhandlung, 1924).

Oswald Spengler, *Politische Schriften* (Munich: Beck, 1933).

Michael Stolleis, *Geschichte des öffentlichen Rechts in Deutschland, Bd. 3* (Munich: C.H. Beck, 2017).

Jacob Taubes (ed.), *Religionstheorie und Politische Theologie*, Band I: *Der Fürst dieser Welt; Carl Schmitt und die Folgen* (2., verbesserte Auflage) (Munich/Paderborn/Vienna/Zurich: Wilhelm Fink Verlag/Verlag Ferdinand Schöningh, 1985 [1983]).

Jacob Taubes, *Ad Carl Schmitt; Gegenstrebige Fügung* (Berlin: Merve Verlag, 1987).

Martin Tielke, *Der stille Bürgerkrieg, Ernst Jünger und Carl Schmitt im Dritten Reich* (Berlin: Landt Verlag, 2007).

Martin Tielke, "Die Bibliothek Carl Schmitt," Carl Schmitt Gesellschaft, Stand 1.6.2015 [http://www.carl-sc hmitt.de/download/biblio-cs.pdf, accessed 26 June 2015].

Piet Tommissen (ed.), *Schmittiana, Beiträge zu Leben und Werk Carl Schmitts*, Band V (Berlin: Duncker & Humblot, 1996).

Gustav Adolf Walz, *Das Ende der Zwischenverfassung* (Stuttgart: Verlag von W. Kohlhammer, 1933).

Max Weber, *Gesammelte Politische Schriften* (Tübingen: Mohr Siebeck, 1980 [Fourth Edition]).

Works Consulted: Secondary Literature on Schmitt in English

Gopal Balakrishnan, *The Enemy; An Intellectual Portrait of Carl Schmitt* (London and New York: Verso, 2000).

Joseph Bendersky, "The Expendable Kronjurist: Carl Schmitt and National Socialism, 1933–36," *Journal of Contemporary History* 14, no. 2 (1979), pp. 309–28.

Joseph W. Bendersky, *Carl Schmitt: Theorist for the Reich* (Princeton: Princeton University Press, 1983).

Stefan Berger, "Prussia in History and Historiography from the Nineteenth to the Twentieth Centuries," in *Modern Prussian History 1830–1947*, ed. Philip Dwyer (Essex: Longman, 2001), pp. 21–42.

Christopher L. Connery, "Ideologies of Land and Sea: Alfred Thayer Mahan, Carl Schmitt, and the Shaping of Global Myth Elements," in *boundary 2* 28, no. 2 (Summer 2001), pp. 173–201.

Joshua Derman, "Carl Schmitt on Land and Sea," *History of European Ideas* 37 (2011), pp. 181–189.

David Durst, "Translator's Introduction," in Ernst Jünger, *On Pain* (New York: Telos, 2008), pp. xxvii–xlvii.

David Dyzenhaus, *Legality and Legitimacy; Carl Schmitt, Hans Kelsen, and Hermann Heller in Weimar* (Oxford: Oxford University Press, 1997).

David Dyzenhaus (ed.), *Law as Politics; Carl Schmitt's Critique of Liberalism* (Durham, NC: Duke University Press, 1998).

Stuart Elden, "Reading Schmitt Geopolitically; Nomos, Territory and *Großraum*," in *Spatiality, Sovereignty, and Carl Schmitt; Geographies of the Nomos*, ed. Stephen Legg (London: Routledge, 2011), pp. 91–105.

Peter E. Gordon and John P. McCormick (eds.), *Weimar Thought; A Contested Legacy* (Princeton: Princeton University Press, 2013).

Rafael Gross, *Carl Schmitt and the Jews; The "Jewish Question," the Holocaust, and German Legal Theory* (tr. Joel Golb) (Madison, WI: University of Wisconsin Press, 2007).

Graham Hammill and Julia Reinhard Lupton (eds.), *Political*

Theology and Early Modernity (Chicago: University of Chicago Press, 2012).

Michael Hoelzl and Graham Ward, "Editor's Introduction," in Carl Schmitt, *Political Theology II; The Myth of the Closure of Any Political Theology* (trs. Michael Hoelzl and Graham Ward) (Cambridge, UK: Polity Press, 2008), pp. 1–29.

Michael Hoelzl and Graham Ward, "Introduction," in Carl Schmitt, *Dictatorship; From the Origin of the Modern Concept of Sovereignty to Proletarian Class Struggle* (trs. Michael Hoelzl and Graham Ward) (Cambridge, UK: Polity Press, 2014), pp. x–xxix.

William Hooker, *Carl Schmitt's International Thought; Order and Orientation* (Cambridge, UK: Cambridge University Press, 2009).

Robert Howse, "From Legitimacy to Dictatorship – and Back Again: Leo Strauss's Critique of the Anti-Liberalism of Carl Schmitt," in *Law as Politics; Carl Schmitt's Critique of Liberalism*, ed. David Dyzenhaus (Durham, NC: Duke University Press, 1998), pp. 56–91.

Nasser Hussain, "Air Power," in *Spatiality, Sovereignty, and Carl Schmitt; Geographies of the Nomos*, ed. Stephen Legg (London: Routledge, 2011), pp. 144–150.

Victoria Kahn, "Hamlet or Hecuba: Carl Schmitt's Decision," *Representations* 83 (Summer 2003), pp. 67–96.

Victoria Kahn, *The Future of Illusion; Political Theology and Early Modern Texts* (Chicago: University of Chicago Press, 2014).

Duncan Kelly, *The State of the Political* (Oxford: Oxford University Press, 2003).

Duncan Kelly, "Carl Schmitt's Political Theory of Dictatorship," in *The Oxford Handbook of Carl Schmitt*, ed. Jens Meierhenrich and Oliver Simons (Oxford: Oxford University Press, 2017).

Ellen Kennedy, "Introduction: Carl Schmitt's *Parlamentarismus* in Its Historical Context," in Carl Schmitt, *The Crisis of Parliamentary Democracy* (tr. Ellen Kennedy) (Cambridge, MA: The MIT Press, 1988 [1985]), pp. xiii–l.

Ellen Kennedy, "Carl Schmitt and the Frankfurt School," *Telos:*

A Journal of Post-Critical Thought, no. 71 (Spring 1987), pp. 37–66.

Ellen Kennedy, *Constitutional Failure: Carl Schmitt in Weimar* (Durham, NC: Duke University Press, 2004).

John P. McCormick, *Carl Schmitt's Critique of Liberalism; Against Politics as Technology* (Cambridge, UK: Cambridge University Press, 1997).

John P. McCormick, "The Dilemmas of Dictatorship: Carl Schmitt and Constitutional Emergency Powers," in *Law as Politics; Carl Schmitt's Critique of Liberalism*, ed. David Dyzenhaus (Durham, NC: Duke University Press, 1998), pp. 217–251.

John P. McCormick, "Legal Theory and the Weimar Crisis of Law and Social Change," in *Weimar Thought; A Contested Legacy*, ed. Peter E. Gordon and John P. McCormick (Princeton: Princeton University Press, 2013), pp. 55–71.

Eduardo Mendieta, *"Land and Sea,"* in *Spatiality, Sovereignty, and Carl Schmitt; Geographies of the nomos*, ed. Stephen Legg (London: Routledge, 2011), pp. 260–267.

Svetozar Minkov and Piotr Nowak (eds.), *Man and His Enemies; Essays on Carl Schmitt* (Bialystock: Bialystock University Press, 2008).

Chantal Mouffe, "Carl Schmitt and the Paradox of Liberal Democracy," in *Law as Politics; Carl Schmitt's Critique of Liberalism*, ed. David Dyzenhaus (Durham, NC: Duke University Press, 1998), pp. 159–175.

Chantal Mouffe (ed.), *The Challenge of Carl Schmitt* (London: Verso, 1999).

Jan-Werner Müller, *A Dangerous Mind; Carl Schmitt in Post-War European Thought* (New Haven and London: Yale University Press, 2003).

Jane O. Newman, *Benjamin's Library; Modernity, Nation, and the Baroque* (Ithaca, NY: Cornell University Press, 2011).

Timothy Nunan, "Translator's Introduction," in Carl Schmitt, *Writings on War*, ed. Timothy Nunan (Cambridge, UK: Polity Press, 2011), pp. 1–26.

Timothy Nunan, "Notes on the Text," in Carl Schmitt, *Writings on War*, ed. Timothy Nunan (Cambridge, UK: Polity Press, 2011), pp. 75–76.

David Pan and Russell A. Berman, "Introduction," *Telos* 142 (Spring 2008), pp. 3–6.

David Pan, "Afterword: Historical Event and Mythic Meaning in Carl Schmitt's *Hamlet or Hecuba*," in Carl Schmitt, *Hamlet or Hecuba; The Intrusion of Time into the Play* (trs. David Pan and Jennifer Rust) (New York: Telos Press Publishing, 2009), pp. 69–119.

David Ragazzoni, "Carl Schmitt and Global (Dis)Order at the Twilight of the *Jus Publicum Europaeum*," *Journal of Intellectual History and Political Thought* 2 (2013), pp. 170–191.

Jennifer Rust and Julia Reinhard Lupton, "Introduction: Schmitt and Shakespeare," in Carl Schmitt, *Hamlet or Hecuba; The Intrusion of Time into the Play* (trs. David Pan and Jennifer Rust) (New York: Telos Press Publishing, 2009), pp. xv–li.

William E. Scheuerman, *Carl Schmitt; The End of Law* (Lanham, MD: Rowman & Littlefield, 1999).

William E. Scheuerman, "International Law as Historical Myth," *Constellations* 11, no. 4 (2004), pp. 537–550.

Carl Schmitt, *The Leviathan in the State Theory of Thomas Hobbes; Meaning and Failure of a Political Symbol* (trs. George Schwab and Erna Hilfstein) (Chicago: University of Chicago Press, 2008 [1996]).

Carl Schmitt, "Hugo Preuss: His Concept of the State and His Position in German State Theory," *History of Political Thought* 38, no. 2 (May 2, 2017), pp. 345–70.

Carl Schmitt, "The Forming of the French Spirit via the Legists," in Carl Schmitt, *The Tyranny of Values and Other Texts*, ed. Russell A. Berman and Samuel Garrett Zeitlin (Candor, NY: Telos Press, 2018), pp. 51–90.

Benjamin A. Schupmann, *Carl Schmitt's State and Constitutional Theory* (Oxford: Oxford University Press, 2017).

George Schwab, *The Challenge of the Exception: An Introduction to the Political Ideas of Carl Schmitt Between 1921 and 1936* (Westport, CT: Greenwood Press, 1989 [1970]).

George Schwab, "Introduction," in Carl Schmitt, *Political Theology; Four Chapters on the Concept of Sovereignty* (tr. George

Schwab) (Chicago: University of Chicago Press, 2005 [1985]), pp. xxxvii–lii.

George Schwab, "Introduction," in Carl Schmitt, *The Leviathan in the State Theory of Thomas Hobbes; Meaning and Failure of a Political Symbol* (trs. George Schwab and Erna Hilfstein) (Chicago: University of Chicago Press, 2008), pp. xxxi–liii.

Jeffrey Seitzer, *Comparative History and Legal Theory: Carl Schmitt in the First German Democracy* (Westport, CT: Greenwood Press, 2001).

Jeffrey Seitzer and Christopher Thornhill, "An Introduction to Carl Schmitt's *Constitutional Theory*: Issues and Context," in Carl Schmitt, *Constitutional Theory*, ed. Jeffrey Seitzer (Durham, NC and London: Duke University Press, 2008), pp. 1–50.

Joshua Smeltzer, "'Germany's Salvation': Carl Schmitt's Teleological History of the Second Reich," *History of European Ideas* 44, no. 5 (2018), pp. 590–604.

Peter Stirk, "Carl Schmitt's *Völkerrechtliche Großraumordnung*," *History of Political Thought* 20, no. 2 (Summer 1999), pp. 357–374.

Tracy B. Strong, "Foreword: Dimensions of the New Debate Around Carl Schmitt," in Carl Schmitt, *The Concept of the Political* (tr. George Schwab) (Chicago: University of Chicago Press, 1996), pp. ix–xxvii.

Tracy B. Strong, "Foreword: The Sovereign and the Exception: Carl Schmitt, Politics, Theology, and Leadership," in Carl Schmitt, *Political Theology; Four Chapters on the Concept of Sovereignty* (tr. George Schwab) (Chicago: University of Chicago Press, 2005), pp. vii–xxxiii.

Tracy B. Strong, "Foreword: Carl Schmitt and Thomas Hobbes: Myth and Politics," in Carl Schmitt, *The Leviathan in the State Theory of Thomas Hobbes; Meaning and Failure of a Political Symbol* (trs. George Schwab and Erna Hilfstein) (Chicago: University of Chicago Press, 2008), pp. vii–xxviii.

Miguel Vatter, "Strauss and Schmitt as Readers of Hobbes and Spinoza: On the Relation between Political Theology and Liberalism," in *The New Centennial Review* 4, no. 3 (Winter 2004), pp. 161–214.

Miguel Vatter, "The Idea of Public Reason and Reason of State:

Schmitt and Rawls on the Political," *Political Theory* 36, no. 2 (April 2008), pp. 239–271.

Lars Vinx, "Introduction," *The Guardian of the Constitution; Hans Kelsen and Carl Schmitt on the Limits of Constitutional Law* (ed. and tr. Lars Vinx) (Cambridge, UK: Cambridge University Press, 2015), pp. 1–21.

Lars Vinx and Samuel Garrett Zeitlin, *Carl Schmitt's Early Legal-Theoretical Writings* (Cambridge, UK: Cambridge University Press, 2021).

Max Weinreich, *Hitler's Professors; The Part of Scholarship in Germany's Crimes Against the Jewish People* (New Haven and London: Yale University Press, 1999 [1946]).

Samuel Garrett Zeitlin, "Propaganda and Critique," in *Land and Sea* (Candor, NY: Telos Press, 2015), pp. xxxi–lxix.

Samuel Garrett Zeitlin, "Indirection and the Rhetoric of Tyranny: Carl Schmitt's *The Tyranny of Values* 1960–1967," *Modern Intellectual History* 18, no. 2 (June 2021), pp. 427–450.

Other Works Consulted

David Armitage, "The Elephant and the Whale: Empires of Land and Sea," *Journal of Maritime History* 9, no. 1 (2007), pp. 23–36.

Joseph Bendersky, *A Concise History of Nazi Germany* (Fourth Edition) (Lanham, MD: Rowman & Littlefield, 2014).

Christopher Clark, *Iron Kingdom: The Rise and Downfall of Prussia, 1600–1947* (London: Allen Lane, 2006).

Christopher Clark, *Kaiser Wilhelm II: A Life in Power* (London: Penguin Books, 2009 [2000]).

Christopher Clark, *Time and Power: Visions of History in German Politics, from the Thirty Years' War to the Third Reich* (Princeton: Princeton University Press, 2019).

Lucy S. Dawidowicz, *The War Against the Jews, 1933–1945* (New York: Bantam Books, 1979 [1975]).

Michel Depeyre, "Clerk, John, of Eldin (1728–1812)," *Oxford Dictionary of National Biography*, Oxford University Press,

2004 [http://www.oxforddnb.com/view/article/5618, accessed 13 June 2014].

Irene Diekmann, Peter Krüger, and Julius H. Schoeps (eds.), *Geopolitik, Grenzgänge im Zeitgeist* (Potsdam: Verlag für Berlin-Brandenburg, 2000) (Bände 1.1 und 1.2).

Dan Edelstein, "*Hostis Humani Generis*: Devils, Natural Right, and Terror in the French Revolution," *Telos* 141 (Winter 2007), pp. 57–81.

Richard J. Evans, *The Coming of the Third Reich* (New York: The Penguin Press, 2004 [2003]).

Richard J. Evans, *The Third Reich at War; How the Nazis Led Germany from Conquest to Disaster* (London: Penguin Books, 2009 [2008]).

Richard J. Evans, *Hitler's People: The Faces of the Third Reich* (London: Allen Lane, 2024).

Julien Freund, "Introduction," in Carl Schmitt, *Terre et mer; Un point de vue sur l'histoire mondiale* (tr. Jean-Louis Pesteil) (Paris: Editions du Labyrinthe, 1985), pp. 9–16.

Julien Freund, "Postface: La thalassopolitique," in *Terre et mer; Un point de vue sur l'histoire mondiale* (tr. Jean-Louis Pesteil) (Paris: Editions du Labyrinthe, 1985), pp. 91–121.

Martin van Gelderen, *The Political Thought of the Dutch Revolt, 1555–1590* (Cambridge, UK: Cambridge University Press, 1992).

Milan Hauner, *Hitler; A Chronology of His Life and Time* (Basingstoke: Palgrave Macmillan, 2005).

Heinrich Heine, *Sämtliche Gedichte, Kommentierte Ausgabe*, ed. Bernd Kortländer (Stuttgart: Philipp Reclam jun., 2009 [1990]).

Daniel Heller-Roazen, *The Enemy of All; Piracy and the Law of Nations* (New York: Zone Books, 2009).

Arthur Henkel and Albrecht Schöne (eds.), *Emblemata; Handbuch zur Sinnbildkunst des XVI. und XVII. Jahrhunderts* (Stuttgart: Verlag J.B. Metzler, 1976).

Jeffrey Herf, *The Jewish Enemy: Nazi Propaganda During World War II and the Holocaust* (Cambridge, MA: Belknap Press of Harvard University Press, 2006).

Jeffrey Herf, *Nazi Propaganda for the Arab World* (New Haven: Yale University Press, 2010 [2009]).

Brad Inwood (ed.), *The Poem of Empedocles; A Text and Translation with an Introduction* (Revised Edition) (Toronto: University of Toronto Press, 2001 [1992]).

Ernst Jünger, *Sämtliche Werke in Achtzehn Bänden*: Erste Abteilung: Tagebücher: Band 2: Tagebücher II. *Strahlungen I.* (Stuttgart: Klett-Cotta, 1979 [1949]).

Ian Kershaw, *Hitler 1936–1945: Nemesis* (London: Penguin Books, 2001 [2000]).

Martti Koskenniemi, *The Gentle Civilizer of Nations; The Rise and Fall of International Law 1870–1960* (Cambridge, UK: Cambridge University Press, 2001).

Jaap Mansfeld and Oliver Primavesi (eds.), *Die Vorsokratiker, Griechisch/Deutsch* (Neuausgabe) (Stuttgart: Philipp Reclam jun. GmbH, 2012 [2011]).

Mark Mazower, *Hitler's Empire: Nazi Rule in Occupied Europe* (London: Penguin Books, 2009 [2008]).

David Motadel, *Islam and Nazi Germany's War* (Cambridge, MA: Belknap Press of Harvard University Press, 2014).

Carl Schmitt, *Tierra y Mar, Consideraciones sobre la historia universal* (tr. Rafael Fernández-Quintanilla) (Madrid: Instituto de Estudios Politicos [Series: Colección Civitas], 1952).

Carl Schmitt, *Terre et Mer, Un point de vue sur l'histoire mondiale* (Introduction et postface de Julien Freund) (tr. Jean-Louis Pesteil) (Paris: Editions du Labyrinthe, 1985).

Carl Schmitt, *Terra e Mare, Una riflessione sulla storia del mondo* (tr. Giovanni Gurisatti) (Quinta Edizione) (Milan: Adelphi Edizioni, 2011 [2002]).

Rolf Peter Sieferle, "Die konservative Revolution und das 'dritte Reich,'" in *Revolution und Mythos*, ed. Dietrich Harth and Jan Assmann (Frankfurt: Fischer Taschenbuch Verlag, 1992), pp. 178–205.

Brendan Simms, "Prussia, Prussianism and National Socialism, 1933–1947," in *Modern Prussian History 1830–1947*, ed. Philip Dwyer (Essex: Longman, 2001), pp. 253–73.

Martin Tielke, "Die Bibliothek Carl Schmitt (Monographien),"

Carl-Schmitt-Gesellschaft [http://www.carl-schmitt.de/down load/biblio-cs.pdf, accessed 15 April 2015].

Franco Volpi, "Il potere degli elementi," in Carl Schmitt, *Terra e Mare, Una riflessione sulla storia del mondo* (tr. Giovanni Gurisatti) (Quinta Edizione) (Milan: Adelphi Edizioni, 2011 [2002]), pp. 113–149.

Yves Charles Zarka, *Un détail nazi dans la pensée de Carl Schmitt* (Paris: Presses Universitaires de France, 2005).

Victor Zaslavsky, *Class Cleansing: The Massacre at Katyn* (tr. Kizer Walker) (New York: Telos Press Publishing, 2008).

Index